Drew Provan

iPhone

7th edition
Updated for iOS 11
Illustrated using iPhone X

In easy steps is an imprint of In Easy Steps Limited
16 Hamilton Terrace · Holly Walk · Leamington Spa
Warwickshire · United Kingdom · CV32 4LY
www.ineasysteps.com

Seventh Edition

In Easy Steps Limited supports The Forest Stewardship Council (FSC),
the leading international forest certification organization. All our titles
that are printed on Greenpeace approved FSC certified paper carry the
FSC logo.

MIX
Paper from
responsible sources
FSC® C020837

Printed and bound in the United Kingdom

ISBN 978-1-84078-792-4

Contents

10   Email   159

11   Accessibility Settings   169

12   Solving Problems   177

Index   187

1   iPhone X

iPhone X is the latest iPhone released by Apple, and marks the 10-year anniversary of the iPhone. iPhone X is a sophisticated and highly capable smartphone that is able to make calls, send texts and multimedia messages, browse the web, take and store videos and still photos, play games, and keep you organized professionally and personally.

The iPhone X comes in only two sizes: 64GB and 256GB models.

The Home button has disappeared but the new gestures are easy to master so you won't miss it (see page 22).

The New icon pictured above indicates a new or enhanced feature introduced with the iPhone X with iOS 11.

The Best iPhone Yet!

iPhone X marks the 10-year anniversary of the iPhone, and there are several major new features not found on other iPhones.

Screen
Now we have the edge-to-edge 5.8 inch display, and the first iPhone to feature an OLED display. This type of display produces incredibly vibrant colors and crispness. The screen adapts to the temperature of the light in the surrounding vicinity. The screen is glass as before, but unique to iPhone X is the glass back of the iPhone.

Cameras
The front-facing (TrueDepth) camera is more powerful and now contains an Ambient Light sensor, speaker and microphone, and a 7MP lens. Using the TrueDepth camera you can create Animojis (animated emojis) to send with iMessage! The rear camera has also been improved and now houses dual lenses.

The new Portrait mode is great for taking photos of people because the background becomes blurred whilst keeping the subject in sharp focus.

No Home button?
This has been removed and many have grumbled about this, but you can access all features using a new range of gestures designed specifically for iPhone X. These are explained later and are easy to learn. Loss of the Home button is no great loss.

Of course, with no Home button there is no Touch ID (where you previously used your fingerprint to unlock the iPhone). Face ID uses biometric information from your face to unlock the iPhone X and enter usernames and passwords in many apps, and is likely to be the standard for future iPhones.

The iPhone knows you are looking at it!
If you are not looking at the iPhone X the notifications will not display preview text. However, if you *are* looking at iPhone X the preview text will be displayed.

Charging and battery life
iPhone X features wireless charging using inductive charging pads. These are available from Apple or third-party manufacturers. iPhone X also features fast charge, and will charge the iPhone X to 50% in 30 minutes. The battery life has also been extended.

What Does It Do?

It would be easier to ask what it *doesn't* do! The iPhone, even as
a basic cell phone before you start adding applications, has many
functions – probably enough for most people, without then adding
more apps of your own. But, since there are *tens of thousands* of
applications available for download from the App Store, you
can extend the functionality of the iPhone way beyond this. The
iPhone is more like a small computer, as you can store files; send
email; connect to other desktop computers; view documents
including Word and PDF files; play games; look up recipes, and
manage your time, as well as many other functions.

The iPhone is more
like a computer than a
standard cell phone.

Apps for work and play   Camera   On/Off button
                                                    (side button)

Settings to customize your iPhone   App Store for more apps

Press and hold the On/
Off (side) button to
turn on the iPhone, or
access screen options
for turning it off. Press it
once to lock the iPhone
and put it into Sleep
mode, or to wake it up
from Sleep mode. You
can also raise it to wake
the iPhone, or simply tap
the screen.

In terms of color, you can get the iPhone X in Silver or Space Gray.

You cannot remove the iPhone battery. This has to be carried out by Apple.

iPhone X Specifications

Processor
The iPhone X uses the fast A11 Bionic chip, which is 70% faster than the A10 Fusion used in the iPhone 7 and 7 Plus models.

Cameras
As before there are two cameras: a front-facing and a rear-facing one. The front-facing camera is a 12MP wide-angle telephoto camera. The rear (called TrueDepth) camera is 7MP, with 1080p HD video recording capabilities.

Cellular and wireless capabilities
The iPhone X uses LTE, and GSM/EDGE.

There is also built-in Wi-Fi (802.11ac) and Bluetooth 5.0. The iPhone also includes Global Positioning System (GPS) software, making it easy to geotag (see page 32) your pictures and videos. The iPhone X also uses 3G and 4G networks where available.

Battery
Unlike most cell phones, the user cannot take the battery out for replacement. The iPhone uses a built-in battery that is charged using a USB connection to the computer or using the Lightning charger supplied by Apple, or an induction charger where you lie the iPhone on a charging mat.

What do you get from a full charge?
- Talk time: Up to 21 hours
- Internet use: Up to 12 hours
- Video playback: Up to 13 hours
- Audio playback: Up to 60 hours

Internal storage
iPhone X uses internal flash drive storage. There is no SD or other card slot so the internal flash memory is all the storage you have – use it wisely!

The iPhone X comes in only two sizes: 64GB and 256GB storage capacity.

What can I do with the storage space?

	64GB	256GB
Songs:	14,000	56,000
Videos:	80 hours	320 hours
Photos:	50,000	400,000

Sensors in the iPhone

There are four sensors in the iPhone: the Three-Axis Gyro, the Accelerometer, the Proximity sensor and the Ambient Light sensor.

The Accelerometer and Three-Axis Gyro enable the phone to detect rotation and position. This is important when switching from portrait to landscape viewing. The Accelerometer is also used in many of the iPhone game apps such as Labyrinth and also the new Dynamic wallpapers (the picture you see on the lock screen and Home screen).

The amount of storage space for songs, videos and photos can vary depending on the way the content has been created, particularly for videos and photos.

The Proximity sensor switches off the iPhone X screen when you make a call – it senses that the phone is close to the ear, saving valuable power. The Ambient Light sensor adjusts the iPhone screen to the ambient lighting, again saving energy if a bright screen is not required.

The iPhone Itself

Unlike some cell phones, iPhone X is unusual since it has very few physical buttons.

Buttons you need to know on iPhone X

- Side button: Sleep/Wake (On/Off)
- Ring/Silent (sound On/Off)
- Volume controls
- Flashlight icon
- Camera icon
- Home bar indicator

Hot tip

Press the Sleep/Wake (On/Off) button as soon as you have finished using the iPhone – this helps conserve battery power, by putting it into Sleep mode. Press the button again to wake up the iPhone (or touch the screen). Pressing the Sleep/Wake (On/Off) button also manually locks the iPhone.

Side button

Ring/Silent switch →

Volume up/down

O2-UK

14:38
Wednesday 31 January

Flashlight icon →

Home bar indicator →

Swipe up to unlock

Camera icon

On/Off/Sleep/Wake

Press and briefly hold this button (or tap the screen) if your iPhone is switched off. This will take you straight to the Lock screen. After using Face ID or your passcode you will then be taken to the Home screen. If you wish to put your phone away, press the On/Off/Sleep/Wake button to put your phone to sleep.

Ring/Silent

You might want your phone on silent, during meetings for example. The Ring/Silent button can be toggled up and down.

When you see the red line, this means the iPhone is on silent.

Face ID

iPhone X uses facial recognition (Apple calls this "Face ID") to unlock the iPhone (unless you have rebooted the iPhone, in which case you will need to enter your passcode). You will know it is unlocked because the padlock icon will change from "locked" to "unlocked".

Swiping up from the bottom of the screen closes any open app, and swiping up again takes you back to the Home screen from any app you are using.

13

Other Buttons on the iPhone

Volume controls

Volume is controlled using two separate buttons – a **+** and **–** button (increase and decrease volume respectively). You can easily adjust the volume of the audio output when you are listening to the Music app, or when you are making a phone call. If you cannot hear the caller very well, try increasing the volume.

There are no visual symbols on the volume buttons: the volume down button is below the volume up button.

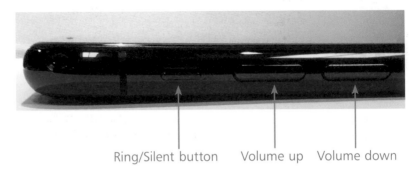

Ring/Silent button   Volume up   Volume down

Nano SIM slot

The iPhone X uses a nano SIM (smaller than the micro SIM used in older iPhone models). Apple provides a SIM removal tool in the iPhone box.

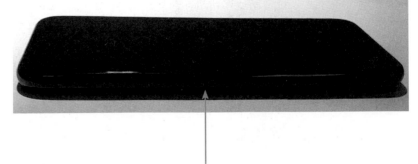

Insert the SIM tool into this hole and push it firmly. The SIM card holder will pop out and you can remove it and insert a nano SIM card.

Lightning connector, speaker and microphone

These are located at the bottom of the iPhone.

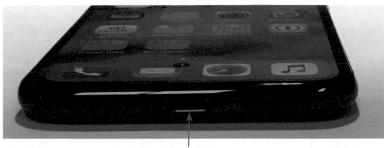

Lightning connector

To charge your iPhone X insert the Lightning cable (illustrated on page 37) into the Lightning connector and insert the USB connector into the plug (both provided with your iPhone X). Then, connect the plug to an electric socket. You can also plug the USB connector to a USB port if you have access to one on a computer. Nowadays, some hotels have USB ports in the rooms.

Back view of the iPhone X

This shows the location of the main camera with inbuilt flash.

Camera with flash/torch built in

There is no headphone/ earphone socket so you will need to use the supplied adapter or switch to Bluetooth headphones.

Wireless charging, where you can simply place the device on a pad or a mat for charging without using any cables, is available with iPhone X. Visit **support.apple.com/ en-gb/HT208078** for the latest list of wireless chargers approved by Apple.

The camera (rear) can capture high quality photos and videos at a resolution of 12 megapixels.

Setting up Your iPhone

Before you can do anything on your iPhone you will need to activate it.

Once you switch on the new iPhone X (press the On/Off button) you will be taken through a series of screens where you set up various options.

Even though the setup is carried out wirelessly, you can back up your iPhone by connecting it to iTunes on a Mac or PC, or backups can be done automatically through iCloud (see pages 62-64).

The setup screens include the following options (a lot of these can be skipped during the setup and accessed later from the **Settings** app):

The selected language also determines the format of the keyboard; e.g. US English or UK English.

● **Language**. Select the language you want to use.

● **Country**. Select your current country or region.

● **Wi-Fi network**. Select a Wi-Fi network to connect to the internet. If you are at home, this will be your own Wi-Fi network, if available. If you are at a Wi-Fi hotspot then this will appear on your network list.

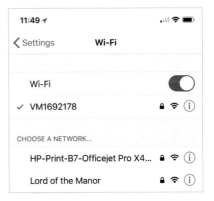

● **Location Services**. This determines whether your iPhone can use your geographical location for apps that use this type of information (such as Maps).

- **Set Up iPhone**. You can use this to set up your iPhone from scratch, or restore it from a backup that has been created via iCloud or on iTunes on a Mac computer.

- **Apple ID**. You can register with this to be able to access a range of Apple facilities, such as iCloud, purchase items on iTunes or the App Store, and access FaceTime, Messages and iBooks. You can also create an Apple ID whenever you first access one of the relevant apps.

An Apple ID can also be created from the Apple website at: appleid.apple.com

- **iCloud**. This is Apple's online service for sharing and backing up content. See pages 52-64 for details.

- **Find My iPhone**. This is a service that can be activated so that you can locate your iPhone if it is lost or stolen. This is done via the online iCloud site at **www.icloud.com**

- **Face ID**. This is used on the iPhone X to unlock the phone.

Face ID can also be used to make payments with Apple Pay, once it is set up. For more details, see pages 44-47.

- **Create a Passcode**. This can be used to create a six-digit code for unlocking the phone. This step can be skipped if required.

- **Siri**. This is the voice assistant that can be used to find things on your iPhone and on the web.

- **Diagnostic information**. This enables information about your iPhone to be sent to Apple.

- **Display Zoom**. This can be used to increase the size of the display so that the icons are larger.

- **Get Started**. Once the setup process has been completed you can start using your iPhone.

The Home Screen

What's on the Home screen?

When you turn the iPhone on you will see some icons that are fixed, such as the top bar with the time and battery charge indicator, as well as the Dock at the bottom that holds four apps. By default, your iPhone X will have Phone, Safari, Mail and Music on the bottom Dock. You can move these off the Dock if you want, but Apple puts these here because they are deemed to be the most commonly-used apps, and having them on the Dock makes them easy to find.

Just above the Dock you see one or more dots. The dots represent each of your screens – the more apps you install, the more screens you will need to accommodate them. The illustration here shows an iPhone with five screens, and the Home screen is the one we are viewing. If you flicked to the next screen, the third dot would be white and the second one would be gray (the first dot is the Notifications screen. In effect, these are meant to let you know where you are at any time.

As you download more apps from the App Store these will be placed on subsequent Home screens, as each one gets filled up.

The default battery indicator is fairly basic. For a more accurate guide, swipe down from the top right of the screen to access the Control Center, which will show battery percentage.

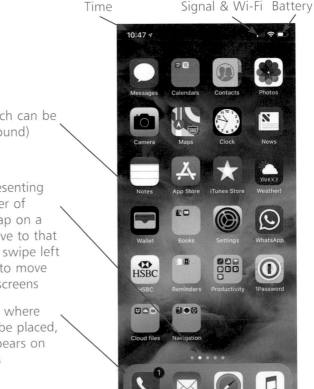

Time

Signal & Wi-Fi Battery

Apps (which can be moved around)

Dots representing the number of screens. Tap on a dot to move to that screen, or swipe left and right to move between screens

The Dock, where apps can be placed, which appears on all screens

Default Applications

iPhone X comes with applications that are part of the operating system. Most of the core set here cannot be deleted.

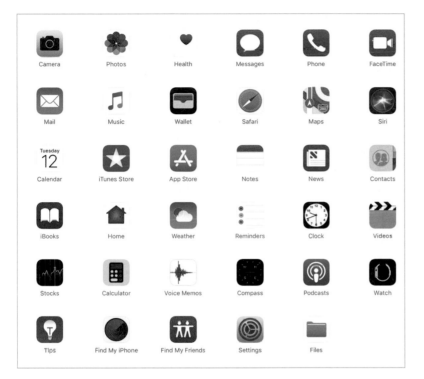

Apple default apps

Many of the default apps cannot be deleted. If you hold down on one app, they will all start to jiggle. You can only delete those with an "x".

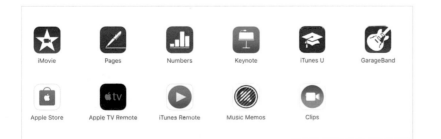

Apple additional apps. These need to be downloaded from the App Store

Other useful apps, such as Apple TV Remote, iMovie, GarageBand, Pages, Numbers and Keynote can be downloaded from the App Store.

The iPhone Dock

By default, there are four apps on the Dock at the bottom of the screen. These are the four that Apple thinks you will use most frequently:

- **Phone**, for calls.

- **Mail**, for email.

- **Safari**, for web browsing.

- **Music**, for listening to music.

You can rearrange the order in which the Dock apps appear:

 Tap and hold on one of the Dock apps until it starts to jiggle

 Drag the app into its new position

 Click once on the **Done** button in the top right-hand corner or swipe up from the bottom of the screen

20

Just above the Dock is a line of small white dots. These indicate how many screens of content there are on the iPhone. Tap on one of the dots to go to that screen.

Adding and removing Dock apps

You can also remove apps from the Dock and add new ones:

 To remove an app from the Dock, tap and hold it and drag it onto the main screen area

 To add an app to the Dock, tap and hold it and drag it onto the Dock

 The number of items that can be added to the Dock is restricted to a maximum of four, as the icons do not resize

 Click once on the **Done** button in the top right-hand corner or swipe up from the bottom of the screen

If items are removed from the Dock they are still available in the same way from the main screen.

iPhone X Gestures

Because there is no Home button on iPhone X there is a range of new gestures to access features on iPhone X. These are key to getting the most out of your iPhone X so it pays to learn these.

Power On/Off
To turn iPhone X On, **press and hold side button**. To turn Off, **press and hold side button + either volume button**. Once slider appears, slide to power Off.

Wake and sleep
Raise iPhone X or **tap** it to wake. To sleep, press the side button.

Use Siri
Say "**Hey Siri**" or **press and hold** the side button. (This has to be set up first – see page 35.)

Use Apple Pay for Face ID
Double-click the side button then **look** at iPhone X.

Unlock iPhone and see Home screen
Glance at iPhone X then **swipe up** from bottom of the Lock screen.

Get to Home screen from any screen
Swipe up from the bottom of the screen.

Multitask (see your running apps)
Swipe up from the bottom of the screen but **keep your finger on the screen** or you can **drag from bottom right** of the screen in an arc, keeping your finger on the screen, and aim for the middle of the screen.

Search iPhone X for anything
Swipe down from the middle of any screen. Type in your search word(s).

Open Control Center
Swipe down from the top right of the screen.

See notifications
Swipe down from top of the screen.

Reach the top (bring items down for easier reach)
Swipe down the bottom edge of the screen.

Scroll between running apps
Drag from left to right along the bottom of the screen.

See widget information
Swipe right from the Home or Lock screen.

Pay using Apple Pay

Switch between running apps

See running apps

Access Control Center

View widgets

Search iPhone X

The Touchscreen Display

iPhone X uses a touch-sensitive screen for input, using gestures and a virtual keyboard. The screen is 5.8 inch (diagonal) and has a resolution of 2436 x 1125-pixel resolution at 458 PPI (Pixels Per Inch). Apple has called this the *Super Retina Display* because the resolution is so high. This results in great clarity when viewing the browser or watching movies on the iPhone X.

Touchscreen features
The screen is able to detect touch from skin, using these gestures:

Tapping
Tapping with one finger is used for lots of apps. It's a bit like clicking with the mouse. You can tap apps to open them; to open hyperlinks; to select photo albums that then open; to enter text using the keyboard; and many other tasks.

Sliding
You can use the slide action to answer phone calls, shut down the iPhone and unlock the Lock screen, as well as to scroll web pages, move to the next Home screen and move between photos.

Dragging
This is used to move documents that occupy more than a screen's worth across the screen. Maps use this feature, as do web pages. Place your finger on the screen, keep it there, and move the image to where you want it.

Pinching and spreading
To zoom in on a photo, web page or map, swipe outwards with thumb and forefinger. Pinch inwards to zoom back out.

Minimizing the screen (Reachability)
Similar to previous iPhones, minimizing the screen (called *Reachability*) needs to be enabled. Go to **Settings** > **General** > **Accessibility** > **Reachability** and turn On. To use this, swipe down on the horizontal bar at the bottom of the screen in any app.

Although the iPhone has a fingerprint-resistant coating it still gets grubby. A number of companies make screen protectors, and you can also protect the other parts of the iPhone from scratching by using a protective case.

Flicking

If you are faced with a long list (e.g. in Contacts), you can flick the list up or down by placing your finger at the bottom or top of the screen, keeping your finger on the screen, then flicking your finger downwards or upwards and the list will fly up or down.

Shake the iPhone

After entering text or copying and pasting, to undo what you have done, shake the iPhone and select Undo. Shake again to select Redo.

Portrait or landscape mode

The iPhone is generally viewed in portrait mode, but for many tasks it is easier to turn the iPhone and work in landscape mode. If you're in Mail, or using Safari, the coverage will be larger. More importantly, the keys of the virtual keyboard become larger, making it easier to type accurately.

Entering text

The iPhone has predictive text, but this is unlike any you may have used before. The accuracy is astonishing. As you type, the iPhone will make suggestions before you complete a word. If you agree with the suggested word, tap the spacebar. If you disagree, tap the small "x" next to the word.

You can shake your iPhone to skip audio tracks, undo and redo text, and more.

To accept a spelling suggestion, tap the spacebar. Reject the suggestion by clicking the "x". Over time, your iPhone will learn new words.

25

Accept the capitalized word by tapping the spacebar

Insert "below" by tapping the option above the keyboard

Double-tap the spacebar to insert a period (full stop) followed by a space, ready for the next sentence to begin.

App Switcher Window

The iPhone can run several apps at once and these can be managed by the App Switcher window. This performs a number of useful functions:

- It shows open apps.

- It enables you to move between open apps and access different ones; e.g. make them the active app.

- It enables apps to be closed (see next page).

Accessing the App Switcher

The App Switcher option can be accessed from any screen on your iPhone X, as follows:

1 Touch bottom of screen and keep your finger on the screen while swiping slowly upwards

2 The currently-open apps are displayed, with their icons above them. The most recently-used apps are shown first

Closing Items

The iPhone deals with open apps very efficiently. They do not interact with other apps unless required, which increases security and also means that they can be open in the background without using up a significant amount of processing power, in a state of semi-hibernation until they are needed. Because of this, it is not essential to close apps when you move to something else. However, you may want to close apps if you feel you have too many open or if one stops working. To do this:

 This gesture differs from previous iPhone models. Touch the bottom of the screen and keep your finger on the screen while swiping slowly upwards

 The running apps have a red "-" at the top left of each running app

 Quit them by tapping the "-" or swiping the app upwards

When you switch from one app to another, the first one stays open in the background. You can go back to it by accessing it from the App Switcher window or the Home screen.

Control Center

The Control Center is a panel containing some of the most commonly-used options within the **Settings** app. It can be accessed with a swipe down from the top right of the screen and is an excellent function for when you do not want to have to go into Settings.

Accessing the Control Center

The Control Center can be accessed from any screen on iPhone X by switching this feature On:

The Control Center is accessed differently on iPhone X. You need to swipe down the screen from the top-right corner.

 Tap on the **Settings** app

 Tap on the **Control Center** tab and drag the **Access Within Apps** buttons On or Off to specify if the Control Center can be accessed from here

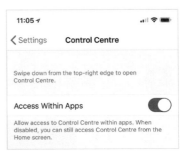

The Control Center cannot be disabled from being accessed from the Home screen.

 Swipe down from the top right of the screen to bring up the Control Center panel

 Tap the screen anywhere to hide the Control Center panel

Depending on your geographic location, some terms will appear with alternative spellings; e.g. Center/Centre, Capitalization/Capitalisation etc.

Use the sliders to adjust screen brightness and volume

...cont'd

Control Center controls

The items that can be used in the Control Center are:

 Use these controls for any music or video that is playing. Use the buttons to Pause/Play a track, go to the beginning or end, and adjust the volume

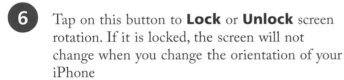

 Tap on this button to turn **Airplane mode** On or Off

 Tap on this button to turn **Wi-Fi** On or Off

 Tap on this button to turn **Bluetooth** On or Off

 Tap on this button to turn **Do Not Disturb mode** On or Off

 Tap on this button to **Lock** or **Unlock** screen rotation. If it is locked, the screen will not change when you change the orientation of your iPhone

 Tap on this button to activate the iPhone's **Torch**

 Tap on this button to access a **Clock**, including a stopwatch

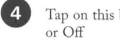 Tap on this button to open the **Calculator** app

 Tap on this button to open the **Camera** app

Hot tip

You can customize the Control Center – see page 38.

Don't forget

When Airplane mode is activated, the network and wireless connectivity on the iPhone is disabled. However, it can still be used for functions such as playing music or reading books.

Hot tip

The Torch function is very effective, particularly over short distances.

Hot tip

The Control Center also includes buttons for Cellular Data On/Off and Screen Mirroring. If you press and hold the panel containing Airplane mode, you will also find AirDrop (see page 109) and Personal Hotspot.

29

The Virtual Keyboard

The keys are small but when you touch them they become larger, which increases accuracy. The letter "t" below has been pressed and has become much larger.

The iPhone has done away with virtually all buttons and provides a software-based QWERTY keyboard. The keyboard becomes visible automatically when needed. When you press on a key it expands so that you can see it more clearly.

There are all the usual features of a computer keyboard, including spacebar, Delete key , Shift , numbers and symbols

To correct a word, touch the word you want to correct and hold your finger on the word. You will see a magnifying glass. Move your finger to where you want the insertion point (|) to be, stop there and delete any wrong letters.

Some keys such as currency and URL endings can be accessed by holding down the relevant key. A pop-up will show further options if available.

The keyboard has automatic spellcheck and correction of misspelled words. It has a dynamic dictionary that learns new words as you type. Some keys have multiple options if you hold them down; e.g. hold down the $ key and you'll see the other characters.

Where's Caps Lock?

It is frustrating hitting the Caps key for every letter if you want to type a complete word in uppercase. But you can activate Caps Lock easily:

 Go to **Settings** > **General**

 Select **Keyboard**

3 Make sure the **Enable Caps Lock** slider is set to **On**

4 While you are there, make sure the other settings are On; for example **"." Shortcut** – this helps you add a period (full stop) by tapping the spacebar twice

11:13	General
‹ Settings	General
CarPlay	>
Accessibility	>
iPhone Storage	>
Background App Refresh	>
Restrictions	Off >
Date & Time	>
Keyboard	>
Language & Region	>
Dictionary	>

11:12	Keyboards
‹ General	Keyboards
Keyboards	2 >
Text Replacement	>
One-Handed Keyboard	Off >
Auto-Capitalisation	⬤
Auto-Correction	⬤
Check Spelling	⬤
Enable Caps Lock	⬤
Predictive	⬤
Smart Punctuation	⬤
Character Preview	⬤
"." Shortcut	⬤

Other settings for the keyboard

- **Auto-Correction** suggests the correct word. If it annoys you, switch it off.

- **Auto-Capitalization** is great for putting capitals in names.

- Whilst the **"." Shortcut** types a period every time you hit the spacebar twice and saves time when typing long emails, if you prefer not to use this you can switch it off. Here's another neat trick – you can also insert a period by tapping the spacebar with two fingers simultaneously (the **"." Shortcut** has to be left On for this to work).

It's a good idea to activate Caps Lock. To use, just tap Shift twice – the Shift button should have a black, upwards-pointing arrow on it with a black bar underneath it if you have activated it properly in the Settings.

If you do not like the default iPhone keyboard, you can download third-party ones from the App Store. Some to look at include SwiftKey, Swype and KuaiBoard.

Camera

The iPhone X has a main camera on the back of the phone, and a second camera on the front. The main front camera is 12 megapixels (MP), and can shoot high-resolution stills and 4K video and 1080p video at 30 fps (frames per second) or 60 fps. The main camera also has a True Tone flash. The front VGA camera is used for FaceTime calls, and can take photos and videos at 7MP (photos) and 1080p HD video.

Both photos and videos can be geotagged, so you can see where in the world you were when the photo or video was shot.

Geotagging helps you determine where the photo was taken, but you need to switch it on in **Settings** > **Privacy** > **Location Services** > **Camera** > **While Using the App**.

Tap on this button so that it turns yellow, to activate Live Photos. This is a short animated clip that is captured in normal Photo mode by tapping on the button in Step 2. It creates a short movie file that can be played in the Photos app by pressing and holding on it, or you can send it to someone as a video. Tap on the button again to deactivate Live Photos.

The Portrait option creates stunning portraits of people. It does this by blurring the background whilst keeping the subject in sharp focus, creating a truly professional portrait picture.

1 Swipe left and right here to move between standard Photo mode, Portrait mode, Square mode, Panorama, Video, Time-lapse and Slo-Mo

2 Tap on this button to take a photo

3 Tap on this button to toggle between the front- and back-facing cameras

The iPhone X front camera has an improved autofocus system, improved face detection and image stabilization for improved clarity.

4 Tap on this button to select a filter effect to add to the photo you are going to take

The iPhone TrueDepth (back) camera can capture high quality video at 1080p standard.

Shooting video

Select the Video option as shown in Step 1 and you will see a Record button (red circle). Press to record video then press again to stop recording.

See pages 110-118 for how to view and edit photos and videos you have taken.

33

Searching with Spotlight

If you want to find things on your iPhone X, there is a built-in search engine: Spotlight. This can search over numerous items on your iPhone, including messages, emails, websites, apps, documents, restaurants and other amenities in your area. It is a powerful search engine very similar to Spotlight on the Mac.

Accessing Spotlight

The Spotlight Search box can be accessed from any screen by pressing and swiping downwards on any free area of the Home screen. This also activates the keyboard. Enter the search keywords into the Search box at the top of the window. Swipe up the page to view the range of results (the keyboard disappears when you swipe up the page).

If you are using it to find an app, tap the app's icon to open it.

In the example below on the left, typing in "app" to Spotlight brings up some suggestions. Typing the full word "Apple" brings up several items Spotlight has found, including emails that mention "Apple".

To return to the Home screen from the Search page, swipe up from the bottom of the screen or tap anywhere on the screen.

Enter the name of an app into the Spotlight Search box and tap on the result to launch the app from here.

Spotlight can search over a range of areas, including nearby restaurants, movies and locations.

Searching with Siri

Siri is the iPhone digital voice assistant that provides answers to a variety of questions by looking at your iPhone and also web services. Initially, Siri can be set up within the **Settings** app:

 Go to **Settings** then tap on the **Siri & Search** link

| Siri & Search | > |

You can ask Siri questions relating to the apps on your iPhone and also general questions, such as weather conditions around the world, or sports results. The results will be displayed by Siri, or, if it does not know the answer, a web or Wikipedia link will be displayed instead.

 Drag the **Listen for "Hey Siri"** button to **On** as well as the other two options if required (**Press Side Button for Siri** and **Allow Siri When Locked**)

 Follow the 5-step setup process to train Siri to recognize your voice

Questioning Siri

Once you have set up Siri, you can start putting it to work with your queries. To do this:

 Say "Hey Siri" or hold down the side button for 2-3 seconds

There are two types of microphone button, shown below. Tap on one of these to ask questions of Siri:

 Ask a question such as, **Show me my next appointment**

 The results are displayed by Siri. Tap on an item to view its details. Tap on the microphone button to ask another question of Siri

Earphones

Apple supplies EarPods, which have a control on the right earpiece cable. This control houses the microphone needed for phone conversations when the EarPods are plugged in. The control also allows the audio volume to be adjusted, to make it louder or quieter.

By clicking the control, audio will pause. Two clicks in quick succession will skip to the next track.

The iPhone EarPods are highly sophisticated and can be used to make calls and also divert callers to voicemail.

Apple has developed new wireless earphones called AirPods. These use optical sensors and an accelerometer to sense when they are in your ears. You can use them to listen to audio and make phone calls. AirPods can be purchased separately, from Apple.

iPhone X does not have a socket for wired headphones or earphones but Apple do supply an adapter if you wish to used wired earphones.

36

Press here ONCE to pause audio or answer a call
(press again at the end of a call)
To decline a call, press and hold for approximately two seconds
To switch to incoming or on-hold call, press once
Press here TWICE to skip to next track
To use Voice Control, press and hold
(this tiny control unit also contains the microphone)

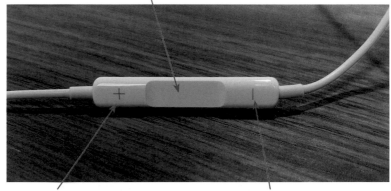

Press here to increase volume   Press here to decrease volume

Uses for the EarPods – this is pretty obvious, but consider

● Listening to music, podcasts, audio books.

● Listening to the radio.

● Watching movies.

● Making phone calls.

● Dictating voice memos.

● Giving voice commands to your iPhone.

Customizing iPhone X

Applications

iPhone X comes with many apps pre-installed by Apple. These can be moved around, or even placed on a different screen, but you cannot delete most of them from the iPhone. These apps are the core features of the iPhone.

The App Store has tens of thousands of apps, which we will look at later. Many are free, while others are available for purchase. With so many apps available for download, the chances are that there will be an app for most things you might want to do.

GarageBand is Apple's music-making app and it can be downloaded from the App Store.

Ringtones

Apple has supplied several, but people will always want to have their own unique ringtone. You can buy these from the App Store or make your own using iTunes or GarageBand. You can assign a specific ringtone to someone in your Contacts list so you know it's them calling when the phone rings.

Backgrounds and wallpapers

Again, there are several to choose from but you can make your own (use one of your photos) or you can download from third-party suppliers. Try browsing the internet for wallpapers or use a specific app. Try out the Dynamic wallpapers! See page 39.

Accessorizing the iPhone

You can use a screen protector to prevent scratches on the screen. There are also many iPhone cases available. These are mainly plastic, but leather cases are available as well. Placing your iPhone in a case or cover helps prevent marks or scratches on the phone.

Headphones/earphones

If you want to use headphones or earphones other than the EarPods provided by Apple, that's fine. You may get better sound from your music but you may not have an inbuilt microphone, which is very useful when you make a phone call. Some headphones and earphones do include a microphone.

USB to Lightning charger cable

With extensive use, the iPhone battery may not last the whole day so you will probably need to carry around a spare charging cable. The USB to Lightning cable means you can plug it in to your PC or Mac at work and charge your iPhone during the day.

iPhone X can use wired or wireless charging. Apple and third parties make wireless charging devices as covered on page 15.

User Settings

There are many settings you can adjust in order to set the iPhone up to work the way you want. These are accessed from the **Settings** app.

As well as the settings already on the iPhone, many apps will have panels for their settings. If an app is not working the way you want, have a look under the Settings Control Panel and scroll to the bottom to see if your app has installed a settings panel.

The **Wi-Fi** Settings are grouped together with those for **Airplane Mode**, **Bluetooth**, **Cellular Data**, **Personal Hotspot** and **Carrier**. Bluetooth can be used to scan for other compatible devices, which then have to be paired with the iPhone so that they can share content wirelessly.

Wi-Fi

Keep this Off if you want to conserve power. Switching it On will let you join wireless networks if they are open or if you have the password.

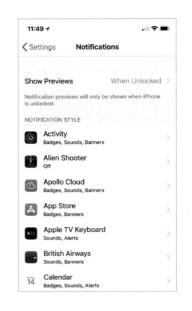

Notifications

This is where you can set what items appear in the Notification Center, which is accessed by swiping down from the top of the screen.

Control Center

This is a set of shortcuts for regularly-used items. See pages 28-29 for details.

Do Not Disturb

Use this to specify times when you do not wish to receive phone calls, alerts or FaceTime video calls. This is useful during the night so you are not disturbed by incoming notifications, texts, etc.

If a Settings option has an On/Off button next to it, this can be changed by swiping the button to either the left or right. Green indicates that the option is **On**.

38

General

This contains the largest range of settings, which can be used to check the software version on your iPhone, search settings, accessibility, storage, date and time, keyboard settings and to reset your iPhone.

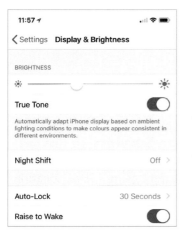

Display & Brightness

This can be used for adjusting the screen brightness, the display viewing size and using larger text sizes, or bold text.

The screen brightness can also be adjusted from the Control Center.

Night Shift reduces the amount of blue light emitted by your iPhone X. This is useful at night and is supposed to make it easier for you to sleep. You can pre-set times for activating this in the Display & Brightness settings. You can manually activate it by going to the Control Center and tapping and holding on the Brightness icon, then tapping Night Shift.

Wallpaper

Wallpaper is the background image you see on the locked and unlocked screens of the iPhone. You can use different images for the locked and unlocked screens. Use your own images or download from third-party suppliers.

Try out the Dynamic wallpapers supplied by Apple. They move as you tilt the phone and are beautiful. Find them in **Settings** > **Wallpaper** > **Choose a New Wallpaper**.

39

You can assign specific ringtones to selected contacts.

Sounds & Haptics

You can place the phone on vibrate or have the ringtone On. You can assign different tones for different contacts.

Face ID & Passcode

This can be used to set up security for unlocking your iPhone and also a numerical passcode (see page 43 for more details).

Battery

This can be used to put the iPhone into low power mode to save power, and view battery usage for specific apps.

One of the iCloud functions is the iCloud Keychain (**Settings > Apple ID > iCloud > Keychain**). If this is enabled, it can keep all of your passwords and credit card information up-to-date across multiple devices and remember them when you use them on websites. The information is encrypted and controlled through your Apple ID.

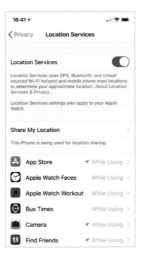

Privacy

This contains a number of privacy options, including activating **Location Services**, so that apps such as Maps and Siri can use your location, using GPS. Location Services also has to be turned On if you want to use the **Find My iPhone** feature.

iCloud settings

These can be found through **Settings > Your Account** at top of the screen > **iCloud**.

iTunes & App Stores

This can be used to specify settings for the online iTunes and App Store, such as enabling automatic downloads when there are updates to your existing apps or music.

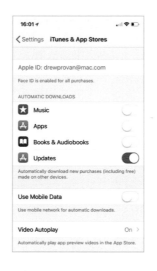

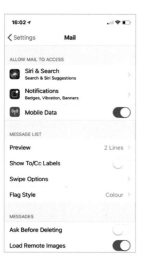

Mail, Contacts, Calendars

Use these three settings to set up email, your contacts list and your calendar.

Apps' settings

A lot of apps have their own settings, including the pre-installed ones. Tap on an app's name in the Settings app to view its own specific settings. It is worth checking Settings after you install an app to see if it has installed a settings file, since it may contain useful features to help you set it up exactly the way you want.

Using the Lock Screen

To save power, it is possible to set your iPhone screen to auto-lock. This is the equivalent of the Sleep option on a traditional computer. To do this:

1 Tap on the **Settings** app

Settings

You can also lock the iPhone using the **On/Off** button on the right-hand side of the phone. Press once to lock, and press again to display the Lock screen.

2 Tap on the **Display & Brightness** tab

3 Tap on the **Auto-Lock** link

Auto-Lock	30 Seconds >

4 Tap on the time of non-use after which you wish the screen to be locked

11:59 ✓ •⎯⎯ 📶 🔋

‹ Display & Brightness **Auto-Lock**

30 Seconds ✓

1 Minute

2 Minutes

3 Minutes

4 Minutes

5 Minutes

Never

Attention is detected when you are looking at the screen. When attention is detected, iPhone does not dim the display.

Face ID & Passcode

Face ID

With the disappearance of the Home button came Face ID, which allows your biometric data (your face) to be used to unlock the screen. When you first set up your iPhone X you will be taken through various steps to let the iPhone X learn your facial features.

To unlock the iPhone X simply hold the phone near your face, and the padlock on the screen will change from the "locked" icon to "unlocked". Your Face ID can also be used to enter usernames and passwords on websites and also unlock some apps; e.g. banking apps.

Face ID is new to iPhone X and replaces the fingerprint ID (Touch ID) used in other iPhones.

Passcode

Also at the same time as setting up Face ID on iPhone X you will be prompted to create a six-digit passcode that you will need at certain times (when your phone restarts, for example).

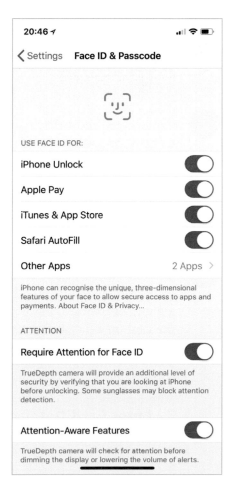

20:46

Settings   Face ID & Passcode

USE FACE ID FOR:

iPhone Unlock

Apple Pay

iTunes & App Store

Safari AutoFill

Other Apps   2 Apps >

iPhone can recognise the unique, three-dimensional features of your face to allow secure access to apps and payments. About Face ID & Privacy...

ATTENTION

Require Attention for Face ID

TrueDepth camera will provide an additional level of security by verifying that you are looking at iPhone before unlocking. Some sunglasses may block attention detection.

Attention-Aware Features

TrueDepth camera will check for attention before dimming the display or lowering the volume of alerts.

You can disable Face ID in an emergency; e.g. if someone is forcing you to unlock your iPhone X using Face ID. Simply press the side button five times to disable Face ID. Unlocking the iPhone X can then only be achieved by using your passcode.

About Apple Pay

Apple Pay is Apple's service for mobile, contactless payment. It can be used by adding credit, debit and store cards to your iPhone X, via the Wallet app, and then paying for items by using your Face ID as authorization for payment. Credit, debit and store cards have to be issued by banks or retailers who support Apple Pay, but there are an increasing number that do so, with more joining on a regular basis. Outlets also have to support Apple Pay but this too is increasing and, given the success of the iPhone, is likely to grow at a steady rate.

Setting up Apple Pay

To use Apple Pay you have to add your cards to your iPhone X:

Cards can also be added to the Wallet at any time from **Settings** > **Wallet & Apple Pay** > **Add Credit or Debit Card**.

If your bank does not yet support Apple Pay then you will not be able to add your credit or debit card details into the Wallet app.

1 Go to **Settings** > **Wallet & Apple Pay** or open the **Wallet** app and tap the **+** symbol

2 Tap once on the **Add Credit or Debit Card** then tap **Continue**

3 The card details can be added to the Wallet app by taking a photo of the card. Place the card on a flat surface and position it within the white box. The card number is then added automatically. Alternatively, tap once on the **Enter Card Details Manually** link

4 Tap once on the **Next** button to verify your card details (ensure the name is exactly the same as it appears on the card)

5 Add any additional details for the card (such as expiration date and the security code) and tap once on the **Next** button. (If the card has already been registered for use on iTunes, the details will be shown here)

6 You will then be sent a code by Apple to verify your card. You should add the code to verify your card

7 Your card will then be added to the Wallet app and you can use it as a method of payment

8 If you have an Apple Watch you will be asked if you wish to add the card to Apple Pay on the Apple Watch

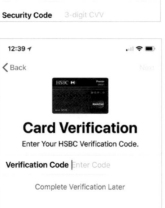

Obtaining your card number using the camera is not always completely accurate. Take the photo in good light and always check the number afterwards and amend it if necessary.

During the setup process you will also have to **Agree** to the Apple Pay Terms and Conditions.

...cont'd

Although no form of contactless payment is 100% secure, Apple Pay does offer some security safeguards. One is that no card information is passed between the retailer and the user: the transaction is done by sending an encrypted token that is used to authorize the payment. Also, the use of the Face ID ensures another step of authorization that is not available with all other forms of contactless payment.

You will be sent a text message, or will receive a phone call, stating the verification code, if selected.

Numerous cards can be added within the Wallet app.

9 Before you can use Apple Pay, your bank or store card issuer has to verify your card. This can be done either by a text message or a phone call. Select the preferred method and tap once on the **Next** button

10 If you selected to verify your card with a text message you will be sent a code to verify your card, as in Step 7. Enter this, and tap once on the **Next** button. Once this has been done, the card will be activated. Tap once on the **Done** button on the Card Activated screen

11 Details of the card that has been added to the Wallet are displayed. This will be visible when you open the Wallet app, ready for use with Apple Pay

Using Apple Pay

Once credit, debit and store cards have been added to the Wallet app and authorized by the issuer, they can be used with Apple Pay in participating outlets. To do this:

1 When you go to pay for an item, open the **Wallet** app and tap once on the card you want to use. Double-click the side button, then glance at the iPhone X to authenticate Face ID

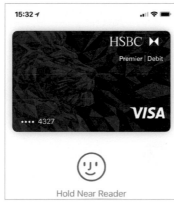

Cards for Apple Pay can be accessed directly from the Lock screen, if this has been set up: **Settings** > **Wallet & Apple Pay** and turn On **Double-Click Side Button**.

2 Hold your iPhone X up to the contactless payment card reader. (Retailers must have a contactless card reader in order for Apple Pay to be used.) The payment should be processed

Apple Pay can also be used on some online sites, in which case the Apple Pay logo will be displayed.

3 To view your payments, tap once on the Wallet app and select a card. The latest transaction is displayed, but not specific items that you have bought. This information is only visible to you and is not shared with Apple. Select **Settings** > **Wallet & Apple Pay** to view a longer list of transactions

LAST TRANSACTION
Costa Coffee N11   £3.65
16/01/2018 - London, England

The Wallet app can also be used to scan items such as boarding passes and cinema tickets, and then used from the Lock screen. However, this can only be done with participating organizations.

Using 3D Touch

One of the innovations on the iPhone is 3D Touch. This can be used to activate different options for certain apps, depending on the strength with which you press on an item. For instance, a single press, or tap, can be used to open an app. However, if you press harder on the app then different options appear. This can be used for Quick Actions, and Peek and Pop.

Quick Actions

These are some of the Quick Actions that can be accessed with 3D Touch:

Accessing the 3D Touch features requires specific extra pressure: it is not just a case of pressing with the same amount of pressure for a longer time. This is known as pressing "deeper" on an app. This also provides a slight buzzing vibration, known as haptic feedback.

Most apps that have 3D Touch Quick Actions functionality are the pre-installed Apple ones. Some third-party apps also support this; most notably social media apps such as Facebook and Twitter. Experiment by pressing deeper on different apps to see if they have options for 3D Touch.

1 Press deeper into the **Camera** app to access options for taking a selfie or recording a video, a slo-mo shot or a regular photo

2 Press deeper into the **Messages** app to access options for sending a text message to recent contacts or create a new message

3 Press deeper into the **Mail** app to access options for accessing your Inbox, adding a VIP, searching for an email or creating a new email

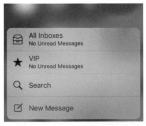

Peek and Pop

3D Touch can also be used to view items within apps, with a single press. This is known as Peek and Pop. To use this, with the Mail app:

Other apps that offer Quick Actions include: Notes, Safari, Music, Maps and Wallet.

 Press on an email in your Inbox to peek at it; i.e. view it with the other items blurred out

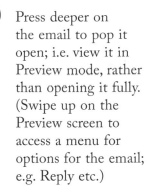

2 Press deeper on the email to pop it open; i.e. view it in Preview mode, rather than opening it fully. (Swipe up on the Preview screen to access a menu for options for the email; e.g. Reply etc.)

3 Press deeper again on the email to open it fully in the Mail app and access its full functionality

Other apps that offer Peek and Pop include: Safari, Maps, Camera and Photos. Items for Safari and Maps can be peeked at and accessed from within an email; e.g. if there is a website link in an email, press it once to view a preview of the web page, and press deeper to open it in Safari. Photos can be peeked at from the Camera app by pressing on a thumbnail image and then pressing deeper to open it.

Data Roaming

Most of us travel abroad for business or pleasure. We like to take our cell phones to keep in touch with friends, family and the office. Call charges are much higher from overseas, and if you want to receive data (email, browse the web, and other activities) you will need to switch on Data Roaming.

Switch on Data Roaming

1 Go to **Settings** > **Mobile Data** > **Mobile Data Options**

2 Switch **Data Roaming** On if required

3 Switch Off when not needed

But beware – the cost of receiving data is very high and will be added to your phone bill. Your standard data package with your network supplier (e.g. AT&T, O2 etc.) will not cover the cost of downloading data using foreign networks!

Data Roaming allows you to receive data when away from your home country, but it can be very expensive.

The cost of roaming in Europe has been capped at a reasonable amount but other countries are very expensive.

Some mobile providers will include free roaming in many countries worldwide as part of their data package.

50

2 iPhone X and iCloud

iCloud is Apple's online storage and backup service. This chapter shows how to set up an iCloud account and use it to save your content and make it available on any other iCloud-enabled devices you have. It also covers sharing your photos, music, books and apps with family members, using the Family Sharing feature.

iCloud and an Apple ID

Apple iCloud

iCloud allows you to use the cloud to back up and sync your data (calendars, contacts, mail, Safari bookmarks, and notes) wirelessly.

Once you are registered and set up, any entries or deletions to Calendars and other apps are reflected in all devices using iCloud.

An Apple ID is required for using iCloud, and this can be obtained online at **https://appleid.apple.com/** or you can create an Apple ID when you first access an app on your iPhone that requires this for use. It is free to create an Apple ID and a username and password are required. Once you have created an Apple ID you can then use the full range of iCloud services.

Start using iCloud on the iPhone and computers

The iPhone apps that require an Apple ID to access their full functionality include: iTunes Store, App Store, Messages, iBooks, Game Center and FaceTime.

 On your iPhone, open **Settings > Apple ID > iCloud** and select the items you want to be used by iCloud. All of the selected items will have their data saved to iCloud so that it is backed up. You will also be able to access these items from other iCloud-enabled devices, such as a computer (see below)

Using iCloud removes the need to sync items such as contacts, calendars, notes and photos on other iCloud-enabled devices that you have, such as tablets and computers: iCloud does it all automatically.

 On your computer, open the iCloud System Preferences (Mac) or Control Panel (PC)

 Log into your iCloud account with your Apple ID (you only need to do this once – it will remember your details)

Check **On** the items that you want to use with iCloud

Using iCloud online

Once you have created an Apple ID you will automatically have an iCloud account. This can be used to sync your data from your iPhone and you can also access your content online from the iCloud website at **www.icloud.com**

 Enter your Apple ID details

 Click on the **iCloud** button from any section to go to other areas

 The full range of iCloud apps is displayed, including those for Pages, Numbers and Keynote

iCloud lets you sync emails, contacts, calendars and other items wirelessly (no need to physically plug the iPhone into the computer).

About the iCloud Drive

One of the options in the iCloud section is for the iCloud Drive. This can be used to store documents so that you can use them on any other Apple devices that you have, such as an iPhone or a MacBook. To set up iCloud Drive:

1 Go to **Settings** > **your account** and tap on the **iCloud** button

☁ iCloud	>

2 Tap on the **iCloud Drive** button so that it is **On**

The apps that can be used with iCloud Drive are generally Apple's own apps, such as Pages, Numbers and Keynote for productivity. However, other app developers are also making more apps that are compatible with iCloud Drive. These will be displayed in the area in Step 3.

‹ Apple ID   **iCloud**

▣	Home	⬤
♥	Health	⬤
▭	Wallet	⬤
☻	Game Center	⬤
✦	Siri	⬤
🔑	Keychain	On >
⬤	Find My iPhone	On >
↺	iCloud Backup	Off >
☁	iCloud Drive	⬤

3 Once iCloud Drive has been activated, tap on any listed apps so that they can use iCloud Drive

When you have finished editing a file you can export it to iCloud Drive. Tap the ellipsis (top right) then choose **Export > Choose a format > Save to Files**

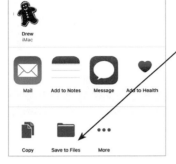

 A Pages document will default to the Pages folder in Files. Tap **Add**. The file will then be saved to the Pages folder

6 In the Settings app, open the settings for the specific app (in this case, Pages). Tap **Document Storage** and make sure **iCloud Drive** is ticked

7 The documents in the app on your iPhone can be viewed on your other Apple devices if you have iCloud turned On and iCloud Drive activated. For iOS 11 devices they can be viewed from the Documents section of the compatible apps (such as Pages, Numbers and Keynote); for OS X Yosemite (or later) devices they can be viewed in the iCloud Drive section in the Finder

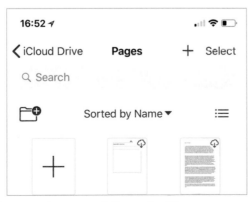

Using iCloud Drive Online

Files that have been saved to your iCloud Drive on your iPhone can also be accessed on any other Apple devices you have, such as an iPhone or a MacBook. They can also be accessed from your online iCloud account at **www.icloud.com**, from any internet-enabled computer. To do this:

If you want to use the iCloud Drive app on your iPhone X you will need to download this from the App Store. **Files** is the new app used to view iCloud files.

 1 Tap on the **Files** app on your iPhone X

2 Your iCloud Drive folders are displayed. Content created within the relevant apps on your iPhone will automatically be stored in the appropriate folders; i.e. Pages documents in the Pages folder, etc.

If you make changes to an iCloud Drive document on your iPhone, the changes will be visible when you open the document on another iCloud-enabled device (e.g. an iPad) with the same app as used to create the document.

 3 Click on a folder to view its contents. You can also edit documents or create new ones with the online iCloud. These changes will appear on your iPhone when the relevant apps are opened

56

Continuity and Handoff

One of the main themes of iOS 11 and iPhone X is to make all of your content available on all of your Apple devices. This is known as Continuity and Handoff: when you create something on one device you can then pick it up and finish it on another device. This is done through iCloud. To do this:

 Ensure the app has iCloud turned On

 Create the content in the app on your iPhone

 Open the same app on another Apple device; e.g. an iPad. The item created on your iPhone should be available to view and edit. Any changes will then show up on the file on your iPhone too

Continuing an email

 Create an email on your iPhone and tap on **Cancel**

 Tap on **Save Draft**

Open the Mail app on another Apple device. The email will be available in the **Drafts** folder and can be continued here

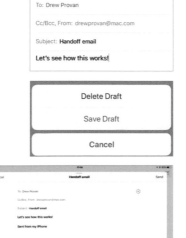

About Family Sharing

As everyone gets more and more digital devices, it is becoming increasingly important to be able to share content with other people, particularly family members. In iOS 11, the Family Sharing function enables you to share items that you have downloaded from the App Store, such as music and movies, with up to six other family members, as long as they have an Apple ID. Once this has been set up it is also possible to share items such as family calendars, photos and even see where family members are, using Maps. To set up and start using Family Sharing:

 Go to Settings > **your account**

 Tap on **Set Up Family Sharing...**

 Tap on the **Get Started** Button

 Choose the first feature you wish to share with your family

 Confirm your account

 Tap **Continue**

7 One person will be the organizer of Family Sharing (i.e. in charge of it), and if you set it up then it will be you. Tap on the **Continue** button (the Family Sharing account will then be linked to your Apple ID)

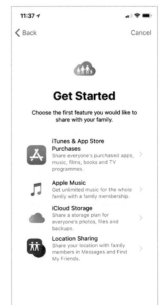

8 Tap on **Continue** again

9 Tap **Invite Family Members**. You will need to sign in to your iCloud account. A new message will appear. Enter the name of the family member you wish to share with

10 Tap **Continue**. You will then see the invitation has been sent

11 Tap **Done**

When you invite a family member you have an option for requiring them to ask for permission whenever they want to download anything from the App Store or the iTunes Store. This is usually done for children that are part of Family Sharing.

Using Family Sharing

Once you have set up Family Sharing and added family members, you can start sharing a variety of items.

Sharing photos

Photos can be shared with Family Sharing thanks to the Family album that is created automatically within the Photos app. To use this and share photos:

 Tap on the **Photos** app

 Tap the **Shared** button

 The **Family** album is already available in the **Shared** section. Tap on the cloud button to access the album and start adding photos to it

 Tap on this button to add photos to the album

 Tap on the photos you want to add and then tap on the **Done** button

 Make sure the **Family** album is selected as the Shared Album and then tap on the **Post** button

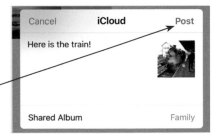

iCloud Photo Sharing has to be turned **On** to enable Family Sharing (**Settings** > **Photos & Camera** > **iCloud Photo Sharing**).

When someone else in your Family Sharing circle adds a photo to the Family album, you are notified in the Notification Center and also by a red notification on the Photos app.

Finding family members

Family Sharing makes it easy to keep in touch with the rest of the family and see exactly where they are. This can be done with the Find Friends app. The other person must have their iPhone or iPad (or other Apple device) turned on and be online. To find family members:

1 Locate and download the **Find Friends** app in the App Store

2 Open the Find Friends app to display all of the active Family Sharing devices. Tap once on a person's name to view their details

and location. Tap on your own name and check that the **Share My Location** button is **On**

To use Find Friends, all family members, or friends, must have iOS 8 (or later) or OS X Yosemite (or later) installed as the operating system on their device. They also need to have shared their location, as in Step 2 here.

Sharing music, videos, apps and books

Family Sharing means that all members of the group can share purchases from the iTunes Store, the App Store or the iBooks store. To do this:

1 Open either **iTunes Store**, **App Store** or **iBooks**

2 Tap on the **Purchased** button (this can be accessed from the **More** button)

 ♪ Purchased

3 Tap on a member of the Family Sharing group

4 The person's purchases are listed. Tap on a category to view those purchases and download them to your iPhone, if required

🔔 Tones	>
🕸 Genius	>
♪ Purchased	>
⬇ Downloads	>

When Family Sharing is set up, a Family calendar is created in the Calendar app. This can be used to add events that can be seen by everyone in the Family Sharing group.

Backing Up with iTunes

iPhone X and iOS 11 are both very much linked to the online world, and the iCloud service can be used to store and synchronize several types of content. However, it is still possible to use iTunes on a Mac or PC to sync content, including:

- Music

- Videos

- Apps

- TV shows

- Podcasts

- Books

iTunes can be used to sync these items (or some of them) onto your iPhone. To do this:

 1 Connect your iPhone to your computer. iTunes should open automatically but if it does not, launch it in the usual way. Click on your iPhone at the top left-hand corner of the iTunes window. Click on the **Summary** tab to view general details about your iPhone

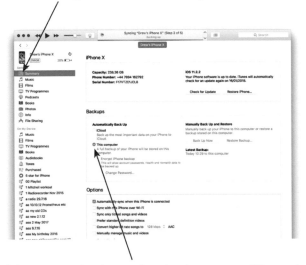

 2 iTunes can also be used to back up your iPhone (in addition to iCloud). To do this, click on the **This computer** button under the **Automatically Back Up** section or click on the **Back Up Now** button

3 Click on the tabs in the left-hand panel to select the items that you want to sync. These include Apps, Music, Movies/Films, TV Shows/ TV Programmes, Podcasts, Books, Audiobooks and Photos

4 Select what you want to sync for each heading (this can be for items in a category or selected items)

When you are syncing items to your iPhone X it is best to select specific folders or files, rather than including everything. This is because items such as music, videos and photos can take up a lot of storage space on your iPhone X if you sync a large library from your computer.

5 Click on the **Apply** button to start the sync process and copy the selected items to your iPhone

6 On the **Summary** page, scroll down to view the **Options** for syncing, such as specifying only checked/ ticked songs and videos to be synced, or manually managing your videos for syncing

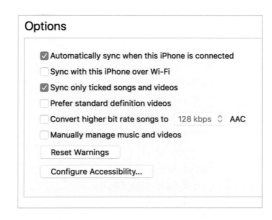

Options

- ☑ Automatically sync when this iPhone is connected
- ☐ Sync with this iPhone over Wi-Fi
- ☑ Sync only ticked songs and videos
- ☐ Prefer standard definition videos
- ☐ Convert higher bit rate songs to 128 kbps ◇ AAC
- ☐ Manually manage music and videos

  Reset Warnings

  Configure Accessibility...

Backing Up with iCloud

Another backing-up option is one that only needs to be set up once and then you do not have to worry about it again, because the backup happens automatically. This is done through iCloud and it can be set up in the iCloud settings. To do this:

1 Tap on the **Settings** app

2 Tap on your account. Click iCloud then scroll down to iCloud Backup

3 Tap on the **Backup** button

> ⟳ iCloud Backup   Off >

4 Drag the **iCloud Backup** button to **On**

5 The iCloud backup overrides any iTunes backups that have been set up. Tap on the **OK** button if you want to continue using the iCloud Backup

6 iCloud will perform automatic backups periodically when the iPhone is locked, connected to Wi-Fi and plugged in, e.g. for charging. Tap on the **Back Up Now** button to perform a manual backup

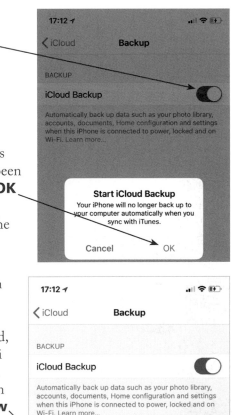

iCloud backups can be used to restore your data when you buy a new iPhone or if you need to reset it for any reason and erase all of its data: **Settings** > **General** > **Reset** > **Erase All Content and Settings**.

If you have a lot of data to back up (songs, photos, etc.) you will have to buy additional iCloud storage from Apple since they only provide 5GB free.

64

3 The Phone Functions

In this chapter we will look at how to use the phone functions to make and receive calls, maintain contact lists and make video calls using FaceTime.

Answering Calls

When you receive a call iPhone X will either ring or vibrate, depending on your iPhone settings. If the iPhone is locked, you will see the name of the caller on the screen and you will need to slide the phone button to the right to unlock the phone and answer the call. You can decline the call by clicking the side button.

If you are using the iPhone when the call comes in (iPhone is unlocked) you will see Accept and Decline buttons. If you do not want to take the call and let it go to voicemail, tap on **Decline** or tap on the **Remind Me** button to be sent a reminder about the missed call at a certain time.

Tap on the **Message** button to send a text message to the person phoning.

After answering a call, the options on the Home screen include: muting the call; accessing the phone's keypad; putting the call on speaker; adding another call; making a FaceTime video call to the person (if they have a compatible device, otherwise it will not be available); and adding the caller to your contacts.

Incoming call, phone unlocked

Incoming call, phone locked

Making Calls Using the Keypad

Although you can do a multitude of things with the iPhone, one of its basic functions is making phone calls. To do this:

 Tap on the **Phone** app

 Select the keypad icon. This brings up a standard keypad on the touchscreen

If you enter a number that belongs to an existing contact, the contact's name will appear beneath the number once it has been entered.

3 Dial the number. This appears at the top of the screen as you add it

You can also select contacts from your Contacts list by selecting the **Contacts** button.

Make FaceTime Video Calls

To use FaceTime

- The caller and recipient must both use an iPhone 4 or later.

- Alternatively, you can use a FaceTime-enabled Mac or iPad.

- FaceTime calls can only be made using Wi-Fi or cellular.

The FaceTime settings

 Tap on the FaceTime app

 Tap on this button to select a contact

FaceTime also has to be turned **On** in the **FaceTime** section of the **Settings** app.

 Select a contact to call. This will be from the Contacts app

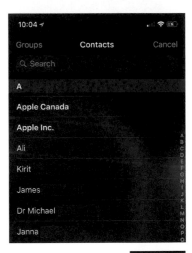

You can also make a FaceTime call to someone by selecting them in the **Contacts** app and tapping the FaceTime icon.

video

 For the selected contact, tap on this button to make the FaceTime call

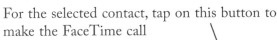

5 While the call is being accepted your own image appears in the main window

6 The recipient must tap **Accept**

If you have already had a FaceTime video call with someone, you can go to **Recents** and make another FaceTime call.

7 Once the call has been connected, the recipient's image appears in the main window

Actions during a FaceTime call

1 Tap on this button to mute the call. You will still be able to see the caller

2 Tap on this button to toggle between the front and back cameras

3 Tap on this button to end a FaceTime call

Using the Contacts List

The Contacts app acts like your own address book on the iPhone:

 Tap the **Contacts** app on the Home screen

 Flick up or down until you find the contact you wish to call. Tap on a contact's name

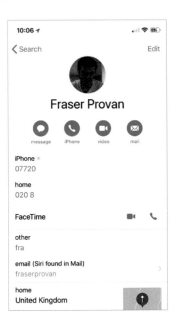

3 Select the action you wish to take; e.g. send a text message, make a FaceTime call, or phone the contact. Tap on the relevant icon to perform that task

The add photo function can also be used to edit an existing photo, or delete it.

Add photo to contact

If you want to assign a photo to a contact, access the contact, tap **Edit** and tap **add photo** (or **edit**) next to their name. Select a photo or take a new one. This gives a more personalized phone call, instead of just seeing a name or a number on the screen.

Using the Favorites List

People you call regularly can be added to your Favorites list. This is the first icon (from the left) when you open the phone application.

To add someone to your Favorites list

 Open **Contacts**

 Select the contact you wish to add

 Tap **Add to Favorites** at the bottom of the window

message	iPhone	video	mail

email (Siri found in Mail)
fraserprovan   >

home
United Kingdom

MSN Messenger
fra

AIM
fra

Notes

Send Message

Share Contact

Add to Favourites

Share My Location

Add the contacts you call most to your Favorltes list.

Depending on your geographic location, some terms will appear with alternative spellings; e.g. Center/ Centre, Capitalization/ Capitalisation, Favorites/ Favourites, etc.

Recents List

Recent calls you have made or missed are listed under Recents.

Missed calls

- These are in the **Missed** tab and are listed in red.

- **All** shows the calls made, received and missed.

- Calls made are shown by this icon.

- Calls received are shown without an icon.

If someone has left you a voicemail message this is indicated by a solid red dot on the **Phone** app and also on the **Voicemail** button on the bottom toolbar of the Phone app. Tap on the **Voicemail** button to listen to your messages.

```
10:07

                All    Missed              Edit

Recents

Larry Provan                   Yesterday  (i)
mobile

Larry Provan                   Yesterday  (i)
mobile

Martin                         Yesterday  (i)
iPhone

Andy                           Yesterday  (i)
mobile
```

To return a call using Recents list

From the names shown in the Recents list, simply tap the name of the person you wish to call.

Assigning Ringtones

iPhone X has a number of polyphonic ringtones built in, or you can buy more from iTunes or even make your own. You can have the default tone for every caller or you can assign a specific tone for a contact.

To assign a ringtone

1 Tap on the **Phone** app

2 Tap on Contacts and select a contact, then click **Edit**

3 Click on the **Ringtone** link

4 Choose the ringtone you wish to assign and tap on the **Done** button

Do Not Disturb

There are times when you do not want to see or hear notifications from apps, or receive phone calls. For example, during the night you may want to divert all calls to voicemail rather than be woken up by phone calls.

 Open **Settings** > **Do Not Disturb**

 Slide the slider to **On** if you want to switch on Do Not Disturb

Allow some callers to get through

You may want to allow friends and family, or those in your Favorites list, to get through and not be diverted to voicemail.

 Open **Settings** > **Do Not Disturb**

 Choose the scheduled time (if you wish to schedule)

 Allow Calls From > choose **Everyone, No One, Favorites**, or specific groups

10:08

‹ Settings   Do Not Disturb

Do Not Disturb

When Do Not Disturb is enabled, calls and alerts that arrive while locked will be silenced, and a moon icon will appear in the status bar.

Scheduled	
From	23:00
To	07:00

SILENCE:

Always

While iPhone is locked   ✓

Incoming calls and notifications will be silenced while iPhone is locked.

PHONE

Allow Calls From   Favourites ›

When in Do Not Disturb, allow incoming calls from your Favourites.

Missed Calls

It happens to all of us from time to time: someone calls and somehow you manage to miss it. If your iPhone was locked when the call was made you can see at a glance that a call was missed, denoted by the red icon on the Phone app.

You can find out exactly when the call was made by looking at the missed calls list:

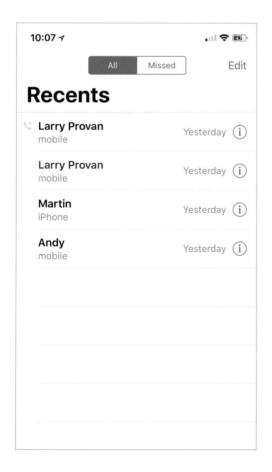

Make the Most of Contacts

The Contacts app on the iPhone lets you call someone, have a FaceTime call, send them an SMS or MMS, email them, and assign them specific ringtones.

message   call   video   mail

Add someone to Contacts

If you get a call from someone who is not in your Contacts list, you can add them from the Phone app.

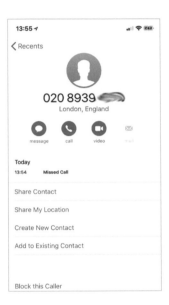

 Open the Phone app and tap on the **Recents** button on the bottom toolbar

 Recent calls and their numbers will be displayed

 Select a number and tap on the information button ⓘ

 Select **Create New Contact**

 Enter the details for the contact and tap on the **Done** button. The contact's details will be added to the Contacts app

Try to enter as much contact information as possible, since this gives you more options for contacting someone.

76

Adding Contacts

You can also add contacts directly into the Contacts app, so you can then access their details. To do this:

 1   Tap on the **Contacts** app

 2   Tap on the **+** button to add details for a new contact

3   Enter the details for the contact, including first and last name, phone, email and address. Tap on the **add photo** button to browse to a photo, or take one with the camera. Tap on the green **+** buttons to include extra items for each field

4   Tap on the **Done** button. The contact's details will be added to the Contacts app

Deleting Contacts

It is relatively easy to delete contacts:

 Tap the contact you wish to remove

 Once their details are loaded, tap **Edit** at the top right

Your contacts can also be accessed and managed through your iCloud online account (**www.icloud.com**), if you have set one up, using an Apple ID.

⊖ MSN Messenger >	fra	
⊖ AIM >	fra	
⊕ add instant message		
Notes		
add field		
LINKED CONTACTS		
⊕ link contacts...		
Delete Contact		

 Scroll down to the bottom of the screen and tap **Delete Contact**

 That's it!

Making Calls Using Earphones

You don't have to hold the iPhone to your ear each time you want to make a call. It is often more convenient to use the EarPods. This means you can keep the phone on the desk and make notes during the call.

The EarPods are very sophisticated – the right cord contains a white rectangular button, which is useful when listening to music – but they are also great for making calls.

How to use the EarPods

Make a phone call	Dial as normal and speak normally. You will hear the caller via the EarPods and they will hear your voice, which is picked up by the inbuilt microphone
Answer a call	Click the middle of the control button once
Decline a call	Press the middle of the controller and hold for ~two seconds (you will hear two low beeps to confirm)
End a call	Press the middle of the controller once
If already on a call and you wish to switch to an incoming call and put current call on hold	Press the middle button once to talk to Caller 2 (and press again to bring Caller 1 back)
Switch to incoming call and end the current call	Press and hold the middle of the controller for ~two seconds (you will hear two low beeps to confirm)
Use Voice Control to dial the number	Press and hold the middle button and say the number or the contact's name

You can use third-party earphones with the iPhone but it is likely you may lose some functionality.

Hide or Show Your Caller ID

Sometimes, you do not want the person you are calling to know your iPhone phone number. You can easily hide your number so it does not display on their screen.

1 Go to **Settings** > **Phone** > **Show My Caller ID**

10:10	
‹ Settings	**Phone**

My Number	+44 7894 ›

CALLS

Announce Calls	Never ›
Call Blocking & Identification	›
Wi-Fi Calling	Off ›
Calls on Other Devices	When Nearby ›
Respond with Text	›
Call Forwarding	›
Call Waiting	›
Show My Caller ID	›

Change Voicemail Password

2 Tap Show My Caller ID **On** or **Off** depending on whether or not you want it to show

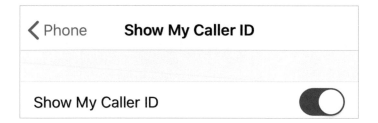

‹ Phone	**Show My Caller ID**

Show My Caller ID	

Call Forwarding

Sometimes, you need to forward calls from your iPhone to another phone (for example, if you are somewhere with no cell phone coverage). This is pretty straightforward.

Setting up call forwarding

1 Go to **Settings > Phone > Call Forwarding**

My Number	+44 7894 >
CALLS	
Announce Calls	Never >
Call Blocking & Identification	>
Wi-Fi Calling	Off >
Calls on Other Devices	When Nearby >
Respond with Text	>
Call Forwarding	>

2 Slide the **Call Forwarding** button to the right (**On**)

10:10 ⏱

‹ Phone **Call Forwarding**

Call Forwarding

Activate call forwarding if you cannot access the iPhone. You could forward to a landline or a work colleague.

3 You will be asked for the number you wish to forward calls to

4 When you no longer need to have your calls forwarded, go back and switch it off

10:11 ⏱

‹ Call Forwarding **Forward To**

020 8412 5635

1	2 ABC	3 DEF
4 GHI	5 JKL	6 MNO
7 PQRS	8 TUV	9 WXYZ
+*#	0	⌫

Conference Calls

This allows you to talk to more than one person at a time and is much like making conference calls using a landline.

Make a conference call

 Make a call

 Tap the **add call** icon on the screen

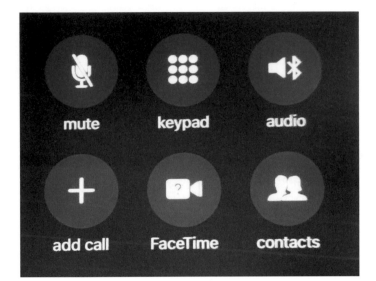

 The first call is put on hold

 Select another contact and make a call to them

 Tap **Merge Calls**

 Now, everyone can hear each other

 Repeat until up to five people are on the same call

Call Waiting

What is the value of Call Waiting? If Call Waiting is switched off, and someone phones you while you are on a call, they will be put straight through to voicemail. However, if Call Waiting is activated, they will know your line is busy and can wait until you are off the call. Or, you can answer their call and put the first caller on hold.

1 Go to **Settings** > **Phone**

My Number	+44 7894	>
CALLS		
Announce Calls	Never	>
Call Blocking & Identification		>
Wi-Fi Calling	Off	>
Calls on Other Devices	When Nearby	>
Respond with Text		>
Call Forwarding		>
Call Waiting		>

2 Tap **Call Waiting**

3 Slide the **Off** button to the **On** position

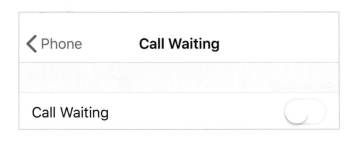

‹ Phone   **Call Waiting**

Call Waiting

‹ Phone   **Call Waiting**

Call Waiting

iPhone Usage Data

How many SMS messages do you have left this month? Or talk minutes? There are times when you need to monitor your usage, since exceeding your limits on your contracted allowance will cost you extra.

How can you check how much you have used?

The iPhone has usage data under **Settings > Cellular Data (Mobile Data)**. The information here is fairly limited in terms of what you have used, or have left, in this month's cycle.

If you exceed your monthly allowance on the iPhone you will be charged extra.

There are some great third-party apps that help you monitor your monthly cellular, Wi-Fi and data usage. Look for these in the App Store.

Most providers have developed their own apps to monitor monthly bills, data usage and calls. Check the App Store to see if your provider has one.

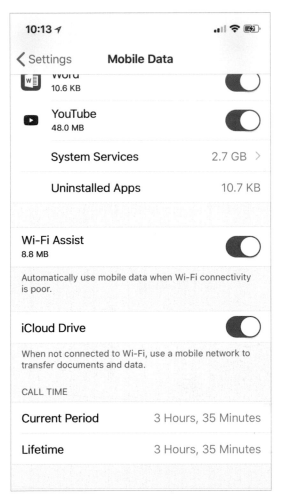

Third-party applications

There are a number of apps that can track your monthly usage. These include *Optus Mobile Usage* for the US and *Allowance* for the UK. Other countries will have their own specific apps.

4 Messaging

These days we text more than we make phone calls using our iPhones. Texting used to be tedious but the iPhone makes it so simple to send SMS messages, iMessages, multimedia messages, and even animated voice messages called Animojis. Here we will look at the full range of messaging options to help you get the most out of your iPhone's texting capabilities.

Text Messaging

Sending text messages on the iPhone X is a fast and efficient way to communicate using your iPhone. You can send messages as SMS (short message service), MMS (multimedia message system – basically text with pictures; see page 90), and iMessage.

SMS

You can send SMS, MMS and iMessages to multiple recipients. Simply add additional names in the **To:** box when you create the message, as in Step 3.

SMS and MMS messages are sent over your mobile carrier's network. iMessages are sent to other Apple users with an Apple ID, using Wi-Fi.

Message settings can be specified in **Settings > Messages**. These include options for sending Read Receipts so that the sender is notified when you've read their message.

1   Tap the **Messages** app on the Home screen

2   Tap the **New message** icon at the top right of the screen

3   Enter a recipient name or a phone number in the **To:** box

4   Add any other names if you wish to send to more than one person

5   Go to the **text box** at the bottom and enter your message

6   Hit **Send** ⬆

7 The progress bar will show you the status of the message

8 Once sent, your message will appear in a green speech bubble (blue if iMessage)

9 Once the recipient replies, you will see their message below yours in a white speech bubble

iMessage

You can send iMessages using cellular or Wi-Fi to other people with iOS devices (or Macs). Simply send your text in the usual way. You will know it's an iMessage rather than SMS because your message will be in a blue speech bubble. You can also check the status of your text message (Delivered or Read) by checking below your message.

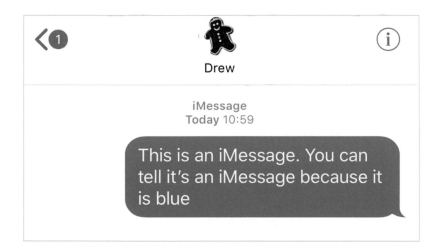

You can tell this message is an iMessage – you see iMessage at the top, plus the text is in a blue speech bubble. You can also see that the message was successfully delivered. If you see the **...** ellipsis in a speech bubble on the left, the person you texted is writing a reply.

Assign SMS messages a specific notification sound so you know you have received an SMS. This can be done in **Settings** > **Sounds** > **Text Tone** where you can select the sound you want to use.

To see how many characters you have used go to **Settings** > **Messages** > **Character Count** > **On**. 160 characters is the limit for one SMS.

Sometimes things go wrong; maybe you entered a wrong digit, and the message does not get sent, indicated by a red exclamation mark next to it. You can amend the number, or tap on the red exclamation mark and tap on **Try Again**.

Using Predictive Text

Predictive text tries to guess what you are typing and also predict the next word following the one you have just typed. It is excellent for text messaging and it is available with iPhone X with iOS 11. To use it:

1 Tap on the **General** tab in the Settings app

General

2 Tap on the **Keyboard** link

Keyboard >

3 Drag the **Predictive** button **On**

Predictive

Predictive text learns from your writing style as you write and so gets more accurate at predicting words. It can also recognize a change in style for different apps, such as Mail and Messages.

4 When predictive text is activated, the QuickType bar is displayed above the keyboard. Initially, this has a suggestion for the first word to include. Tap on a word or start typing

5 As you type, suggestions appear. Tap on one to accept it. Tap on the word within the quotation marks to accept exactly what you have typed

You can switch off suggested words by switching Predictive to **Off**.

88

6 If you continue typing, the predictive suggestions will change as you add more letters

 7 After you have typed a word, a suggestion for the next word appears. Tap on one of the suggestions, or start typing a new word, which will then also have predictive suggestions as you type

Toggling predictive text from the keyboard
You can also toggle predictive text On or Off from the keyboard. To do this:

 1 Press and hold this button on the keyboard

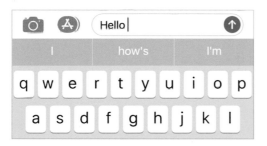 **2** Tap **Keyboard Settings...** that takes you to the settings for your keyboard. Turn the **Predictive** button **On** or **Off**

The button in Step 1 can also be used to add emojis (or smileys), which are symbols used in text messages to signify happiness, surprise, sadness, etc.

Sending MMS Messages

The iPhone can send more than just plain, boring text messages. MMS means Multimedia Message Service, which is basically a means of sending images, including video, to a recipient, rather than a simple SMS message. Each MMS counts as two SMS messages, so be careful how many you send.

To send an MMS

MMS messages sometimes incur charges with cellular/mobile phone carriers. Check with your provider if you are in doubt.

1 Tap **Messages** and tap the **New message** icon

2 Enter the **name** of the recipient

3 Tap the **camera** icon (to the left of the text box)

4 Tap on the **Take Photo or Video** button to capture a new image, or tap on the **Photo Library** button to select an item from your photos or videos

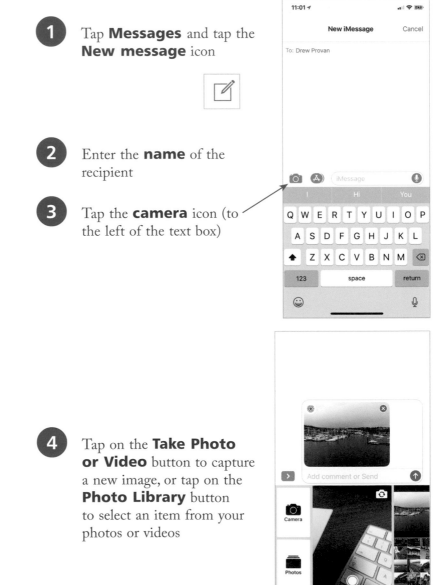

5 Browse to the picture or video you want to send, from within the **Photos** app, and tap on the **Choose** button to select it

6 The picture will appear in the message box

7 Type your text message to accompany the picture or video

8 Hit **Send**

Sending Audio Clips

You can also send audio messages in an iMessage so that people can actually hear from you too. To do this:

 1 Open a new iMessage

 2 Press and hold on the microphone icon at the right-hand side of the text box

 3 Create your audio clip and release the microphone button

4 Tap on this button to add the clip to the message

 5 Tap on this button to delete the current clip and start recording again

 6 If the audio clip is added it shows up in the iMessages area. The recipient can use the **Play** button to hear it

Recipients will need to have a compatible phone or computer in order to play an audio message.

If you want to keep the audio message tap the **Keep** button, otherwise the audio message will disappear two minutes after you listen to it.

Sharing Your Location

With Messages you can now also show people your location (by sending a map) rather than just telling them. To do this:

1 Open a conversation where someone has asked where you are, then tap once on the **Details** button

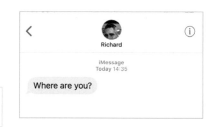

2 Tap once on the **Send My Current Location**, or **Share My Location** buttons

3 For **Share My Location**, tap once on one of the options for how long you want your location to be shared for. These include sharing for an hour, a day or indefinitely

4 Your location is shown on a map and sent to the other person in the conversation

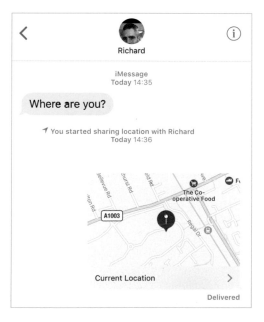

If you select **Share My Location**, this will be updated if your location changes (as long as Location Services is turned **On** in **Settings** > **Privacy** > **Location Services**.

Managing Text Messages

Forwarding a text message

You can easily forward a text message to another person.

1 Open the message, and press and hold on the message

2 Tap on the **More...** button

3 Tap on the **Forward** button and enter a recipient name

4 Tap on the **Send** button

Deleting a text message

1 Open Messages to show your list of text messages

2 Swipe the text message right to left then tap **Delete**

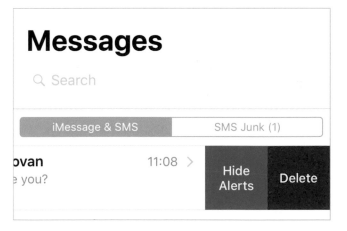

In the App Store there are several apps that let you message friends and colleagues. Examples include Skype, WhatsApp, Viber, and others.

Skype

Viber

Animojis on iPhone X

Apple has created Animojis, which are only available on iPhone X. These are animated voice clips that you can send in messages. The TrueDepth camera analyses your facial expressions and can mirror these as you move your mouth and head as you speak. There are 12 beautifully designed Animojis to choose from.

Animojis are new and only found on iPhone X (*at the time of writing*).

Other special effects are available in Messages. Once you've written your message, before you send it, press and hold the **Send** ⬆ button, and you'll be shown a choice of special effects to select from. When you're happy with your selection, tap the **Send** button again to send the message.

1 Open the Messages app and start a new message or tap an existing one

2 Tap (Ⓐ) then

3 Choose your Animoji from the left-hand side of the screen

4 Look straight into iPhone X and place your face in the frame

5 Tap the **Record** button ●. Stop recording by tapping ▪

6 You can record 10 seconds of sound

7 Preview your Animoji by tapping ↻

8 To send, press ⬆

Live Links

When you send a text message, an email, or use a social networking app where text is inserted, you can add phone numbers, web URLs and email addresses. The recipient can then click on these to return the call, visit a website, or send an email.

To copy and forward a URL from a website:

Phone numbers, email addresses and URLs in messages are live and can be tapped to call the number, view other web pages or send emails.

1 Go to the selected web page in Safari, touch and hold the web address (URL) at the top of the page, then select **Copy**

2 Go to Messages and create a new message. Touch and hold the text box and select **Paste**. Add additional text if required, then press the **Send** button

To copy and forward a phone number:

Live links to phone numbers and email addresses don't end with Mail. You can also use phone numbers in Safari. If you see a number you want to dial on a web page, put your finger on the number and hold until a box pops up showing you the various options. These include calling the number, sending a text message, creating a new contact or adding to an existing contact.

1 Go to the selected contact, touch and hold the phone number you wish to send, then select **Copy**

2 Go to Messages and create a new message. Touch and hold the text box and select **Paste**. Add additional text if required, then press the **Send** button

Live links in emails

If you send an email to someone and include a website, email address or URL these are also clickable.

Click on the link to go to that site in a web browser.

15:05 ✈   .ıll 🗚 📶

< All Inboxes   ∧   ∨

From: Drew Provan >
To: Drew Provan >   Hide

Best computing books!
Today at 15:05

Check out this site

www.ineasysteps.com

Cheers

5 Music and Movies

iPhone X is a workhorse, but is also a fun device, able to play music and movies with excellent sound quality and superb visual quality on the Super Retina HD screen. This chapter shows how to obtain, play and manage music on your iPhone and also view movies and other similar content from the iTunes Store.

The Music App

The Music app can be used to turn your iPhone into your own personal jukebox. To use it:

1 Tap on the **Music** app on the Dock

If you don't like the way the various functions are shown on the Music app, then you can change these. Go to **Settings** > **Music**.

2 Tap on the **Library** button on the bottom toolbar. This displays any music items currently on your iPhone (music downloaded from the iTunes Store; see page 104) or imported into iTunes from a CD, or from the Apple Music service

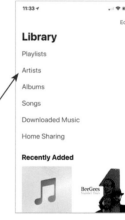

You can create your own playlists in the Music app by tapping on the **Playlists** button at the top of the **My Music** window. Tap on the **New** button, give the playlist a name and tap on the **Add Songs** button to select songs for the playlist. This will then be available from the **Playlists** button.

3 Tap on the **Artists** button to view more options for how you view your music, such as by Albums, Songs, Genres and Composers. Or, you can listen to one of your **Playlists**

Play Audio on the Music App

The Music app is very versatile for playing your favorite albums and tracks. To use it:

1 Tap on the **Music** app on the Dock

2 Tap on the **Library** button at the top of the window and tap **Artists**

3 Tap the name of the artist and choose the album you want to hear

4 Tap on the track that you want to play. If you select the first track of an album then the other tracks will play in sequence after it

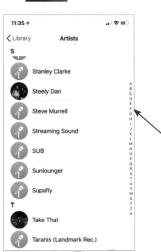

Tap on this bar to search for items in alphabetical order. Tap on the Search icon at the bottom of the window to search for specific artists or songs.

You can play a song from your Music Library by using Siri. Hold down the Home button until Siri appears and then say, "Play, (name of song)" and it should start playing automatically.

Music App Controls

Once a track is playing in the Music app there are a number of controls that can be used.

 Tap here to view the selected track playing in the Music app interface

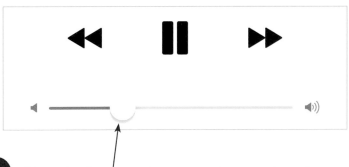

Music controls, including Play, Fast Forward, Rewind and Volume can also be applied in the **Control Center**, which can be accessed by swiping up from the bottom of the screen.

The volume can also be changed using the controls on the iPhone EarPods (see page 36), or with the volume button on the side of the iPhone.

 Tap once on the middle button to pause/play the currently-playing track. Use the buttons on either side to move to the beginning or end of a track

 Drag this button to increase or decrease the volume

 Tap once on this button to repeat a song or album after it has played

 Tap once on this button to shuffle the order of songs on your iPhone

View the Music Tracks

Sometimes you want to see what tracks are available while you are listening to audio, or you want to download tracks.

While viewing the album artwork screen
To view the Up Next tracks:

 Tap on the track playing (bottom of screen). Another screen will open

2 Scroll down till you see **Up Next**

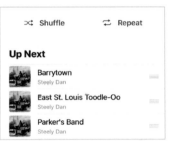

Downloading tracks
To download tracks that have been bought through iTunes on another device (or Apple Music):

1 Tap the iCloud icon to download the track to your iPhone X

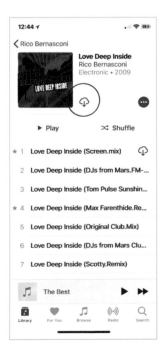

Items that are in your iTunes Library but have not been bought on your iPhone (e.g. bought on an iPad or Mac) are played on your iPhone by streaming over Wi-Fi. This means that the actual item is not downloaded to your iPhone, unless you use the **Make Available Offline** option.

Starting with Apple Music

Apple Music makes the entire Apple iTunes Library of music available to users. It is a subscription service, but there is a three-month free trial. Music can be streamed over the internet or downloaded so you can listen to it when you are offline. To start with Apple Music:

To end your Apple Music subscription at any point (and to ensure you do not subscribe at the end of the free trial) open the **Settings** app. Tap once on the **iTunes & App Store** button and tap once on your own **Apple ID** link (in blue). Tap once on the **View Apple ID** button and under **Subscriptions** tap once on the **Manage** button. Drag the **Automatic Renewal** button to **Off**. You can then renew your Apple Music membership, if required, by selecting one of the **Renewal Options**. If you do not renew your subscription once the free trial finishes, you will not be able to access any music that you have downloaded during the trial.

1 Tap once on the **Music** app

2 Tap once on the **For You** button

3 Tap once on the **Try It Now** button. (Either an **Individual** or a **Family** membership plan can be selected, and your Apple ID password is required to sign in)

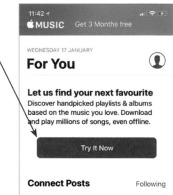

4 Select the types of music in which you are interested and tap once on the **Next** button to move through the process. This will help to populate the **For You** page, which is a selection of suggestions that you may like. You can also search for items using the Search icon at the top of the Apple Music window

Using Apple Music

 Tap **For You** in the Music screen. You can see what your friends are listening to, browse that day's playlist, or search for an artist yourself

 Tap **Search** and enter the name of an artist or band

 Tap on the artist when found by Search

 Tap the ellipsis ⚫⚫⚫ to **Follow, Create Station** or **Share Artist**

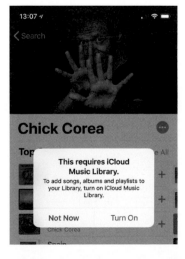 To add tracks to your iCloud Music Library, tap the **+** symbol. The app will tell you that an iCloud Music Library is required. Turn this On and the track will be added to your Library

By default, music from Apple Music is stored within iCloud and this is where it is streamed from. This means that it is played over an online Wi-Fi connection. If it is downloaded, as in Step 2, then it can be played even if you are not online.

For Apple Music to work properly, both **Show Apple Music** and **iCloud Music Library** should be turned **On** within the **Music** section of the **Settings** app.

Buying Music

Music on iPhone X can be downloaded and played using the iTunes and Music apps respectively. iTunes links to the iTunes Store, from where music and other content can be bought and downloaded to your iPhone. To do this:

1 Tap once on the **iTunes Store** app

2 Tap once on the **Music** button on the iTunes toolbar at the bottom of the window

3 Use the buttons at the bottom of the window to view the music content, or swipe up and down, and left and right in the main window

You need to have an Apple ID with credit or debit card details added to be able to buy music from the iTunes Store.

4 Tap once on an item to view it. Tap once here to buy an album or tap on the button next to a song to buy that individual item

5 Purchased items are included in the Music app's Library

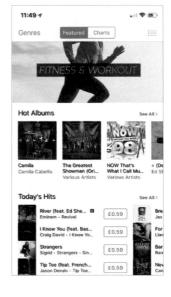

Watching Movies

The iPhone is a great video player.

 Tap on the **TV** app

 To find content, tap on the **Store** button

 Browse the video store to select a title and download it, or watch a trailer

 Select the video or trailer in the **TV** app and tap the **Play** button. The playback screen will automatically rotate to landscape

 Adjust volume, rewind and access other features using the controls that are shown below

If you want to stop, simply press the **Play/Pause** button and it will save your place

You can also watch YouTube videos on your iPhone, by either going to the YouTube website in Safari, or by downloading the YouTube app from the App Store.

You have a few ways of getting videos on your iPhone: home movies, either using a camcorder or the iPhone camera; converting your purchased DVDs to iPhone format; and buying or renting movies from the iTunes Store. DVDs can be converted with an app such as Handbrake, but make sure it is legal to do so first.

Podcasts

The iPhone is also great for listening to audiobooks and podcasts. This can be done with the Podcasts app.

 Open the **Podcasts** app

Catching up with podcasts is a great way to pass the time on long bus or train journeys.

 Tap on the Podcasts app to open it and view the available podcasts (which can be audio and video)

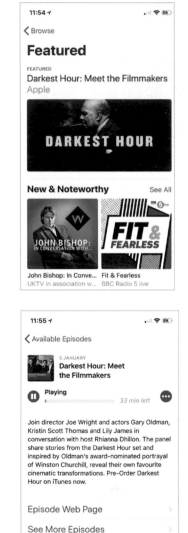

Tap on a podcast to download it to your iPhone

Tap on a podcast in the **My Podcasts** section to listen to it. If a podcast has a red circle on it with a number, this means that there are updates or new versions/episodes available for it

6 Photos and Videos

iPhone X has two superb built-in cameras, and is able to shoot video as well as still images. In addition, you can manage and edit your photos and videos directly on iPhone X itself, with the Photos app.

Sharing Content

Since the iPhone can store and create such a great range of content, it seems a shame to keep it all to yourself, as there are options for sharing all kinds of content. The example here is for one of the most popular: sharing photos, but the process also applies to other content such as web pages, notes and contacts.

1 Open a photo at full size and tap on the **Share** button

2 Tap on one of the options for sharing the photo. These include messaging; emailing; sending to iCloud; sending to a note; adding to a contact in your

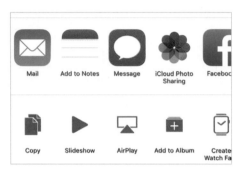

Contacts app; using as your iPhone wallpaper; tweeting; sending to Facebook or Flickr; printing; and copying

3 The photo is added to the item selected in Step 2, in this case an iMessage in the Messages app

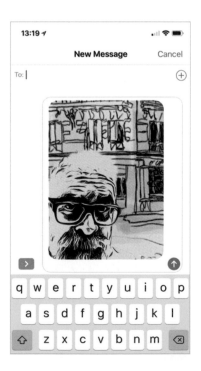

If you share a photo to a note in the Notes app, a new note will be created, with the photo already inserted.

Don't forget you can take panoramic pictures. Open the camera and choose **Pano**, and move the iPhone X as instructed by the app.

Sharing with AirDrop

AirDrop is a feature for sharing files wirelessly with other Apple users over short distances. It has been available on Mac computers for a number of years and is available on iPhone X. To use it:

1 Swipe down from top right of the screen to access the Control Center

2 Tap and hold the box at the top left (Airplane mode, connectivity, Wi-Fi, Bluetooth). The **AirDrop** option will display

Other types of content can be shared with AirDrop, but photos are one of the most common.

3 Select how you want to share your files with other AirDrop users. This can be with your contacts in the Contacts app, or Everyone

4 Select an item you want to share, such as a photo in the Photos app, and tap on the **Share** button

5 If there are people nearby with AirDrop activated, the AirDrop button will

be blue on your iPhone, and will then display icons for the people available

When using AirDrop, make sure you are as close as possible to the other user and that they have AirDrop turned on in the Control Center.

6 Tap on an available icon to share your content with this person (they will have to accept it via AirDrop once it has been sent)

Where Are My Pictures?

As shown in Chapter 1, the front-facing camera can be used to capture photos and video. Once these have been captured they can be viewed and organized in the Photos app. To do this:

1   Tap on the **Photos** app

If you have iCloud set up for photos, select **Settings** > **Photos & Camera** and turn On **Upload to My Photo Stream** to enable all of your new photos taken on your iPhone to be made available on any other iCloud-enabled devices. Turn On **iCloud Photo Library** to make your photos on other devices available on your iPhone too.

2   At the top level, all photos are displayed according to the years in which they were taken

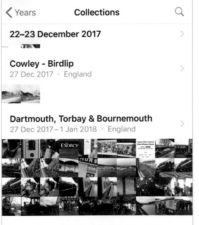

110

Tap once on the **Photos**, **Memories**, **Shared** and **Albums** buttons at the bottom of the **Years**, **Collections** or **Moments** windows, to view the photos in each of these sections.

3   Tap within the **Years** window to view photos according to specific, more defined, timescales. This is the **Collections** level. Tap on the **Years** button to move back up one level

4 Tap within the **Collections** window to drill down further into the photos, within the **Moments** window. Tap on the **Collections** button to go back up one level

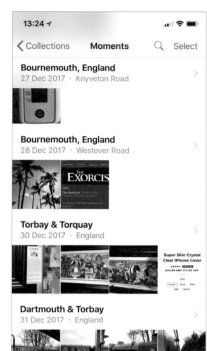

Moments are created according to the time at which the photos were added or taken: photos added at the same time will be displayed within the same Moment.

5 Tap on a photo within the **Moments** window to view it at full size. Tap on the **Moments** button to go back up one level

Double-tap with one finger on an individual photo to zoom in on it. Double-tap with one finger again to zoom back out. To zoom in to a greater degree, spread outwards with thumb and forefinger.

111

Creating Albums

Within the Photos app it is possible to create different albums in which you can store photos. This can be a good way to organize them according to different categories and headings. To do this:

1 Tap on the **Albums** button

2 Tap on this button

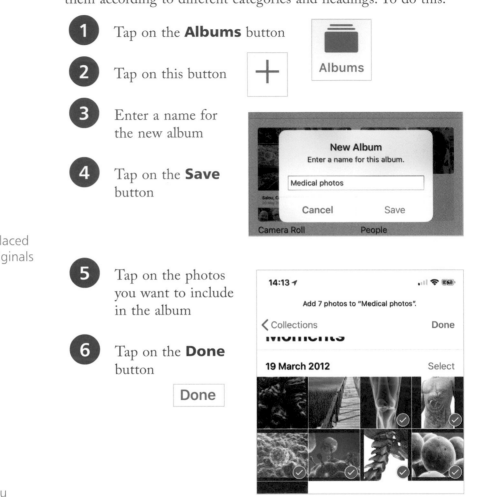

Albums

3 Enter a name for the new album

4 Tap on the **Save** button

New Album

Enter a name for this album.

Medical photos

Cancel   Save

Camera Roll   People

When photos are placed into albums, the originals remain in the main **Photos** section.

5 Tap on the photos you want to include in the album

6 Tap on the **Done** button

Done

14:13

Add 7 photos to "Medical photos".

‹ Collections   Done

19 March 2012   Select

Be careful how you delete photos. If you delete a photo from an album you will be asked whether you want to **Remove it from Album** (photo remains in Camera Roll) or **Delete** (gone from your album *and* Camera Roll).

7 Tap on the **Albums** button to view the album

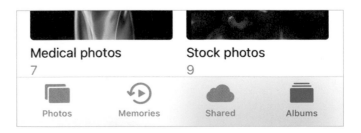

Medical photos
7

Stock photos
9

Photos   Memories   Shared   Albums

112

Selecting Photos

It is easy to take hundreds or even thousands of digital photos, and most of the time you will only want to use a selection of them. Within the Photos app it is possible to select individual photos so that you can share them, delete them or add them to albums.

 Access the Moments section and tap on the **Select** button

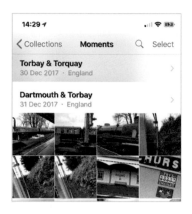

Press and hold on a photo to access an option to copy it, rather than selecting it.

2 Tap on the photos you want to select, or tap on the **Select** button again to select all of the photos

To add items to an album, tap on this button in the **Moments** section.

Select

Tap on photos to select them, then tap on the **Add To** button and select either an existing album or tap on the **New Album** link to create a new album, with the selected photos added to it.

3 Tap on the **Cancel** button if you want to remove the selection

4 Use these buttons to, from left to right, share the selected photos, add them to an album or delete them

Editing Photos

The Photos app has options to perform some basic photo-editing operations. To use these:

1 Open a photo at full-screen size and tap once on the **Edit** button to access the editing tools

Editing changes are made to the original photo once the changes have been saved. These will also apply to any albums into which the photo has been placed.

2 Tap on the **Auto Enhance** button at the top right of the screen to have auto-coloring editing effects applied to the photo

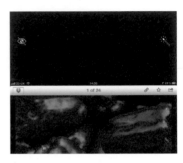

Most photos benefit from some cropping, to enhance the main subject and give it greater prominence.

3 Tap on the **Crop** button and drag the resizing handles to select an area of the photo that you want to keep, and discard the rest

In the Crop section, tap on this button to change the aspect of the photo; i.e. the dimensions at which it is displayed.

4 Tap on the **Rotate** button to rotate the photo 90 degrees at a time, anti-clockwise

5 Tap on the **Filters** button to select special effects to be applied to the photo

 6 Tap on the **Enhance** button to have auto-coloring editing applied to the photo

7 For each function, tap on the **Done** button to save the photo with the selected changes

If you reopen a photo that has been edited and closed, you have an option to **Revert** to its original state, before it was edited.

 8 Tap on the **Cancel** button to quit the editing process

Taking Videos

To capture your own video footage:

 1 Tap the **Camera** icon to load the app. The shutter will open to show the image view

 2 Drag just above the shutter button until **Video** is showing

 3 Tap on the red **Record** button

iPhone X can capture video in 4K format, which is higher quality than High Definition (HD).

 4 The **Record** button turns into a red square during filming

Hold the phone in Landscape mode when shooting video.

Videos are located in the **Videos** album within the **Photos** app.

 5 When you have finished, tap the Record button again. Your video will be saved in the **Photos** app

Editing the Video

You can edit the video you have taken on a Mac, PC or directly on the iPhone itself.

1 Tap the **Photos** app

2 Access the video in the same way as for accessing photos

3 **Tap the video** to open it – the image can be viewed in portrait or landscape, but landscape is easier for trimming

4 **Touch the screen** and tap on the **Edit** button. The trimming timeline will be shown at the bottom of the screen

15:04
‹ Back   1 January
         00:13   Edit

5 Decide what (if anything) you want to trim, and drag the yellow sliders on the left and right until you have marked the areas you wish to trim

6 Tap the yellow **Done** button at the bottom right of the screen and the unwanted video will be removed

7 Tap on the **Save as New Clip** button to save the edited clip

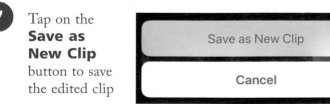

Save as New Clip

Cancel

Video editing is now non-destructive, which means you can trim your video, but the original video clip is left intact.

117

Have Fun with Clips!

iOS 11 brings with it Clips, a fun video app that lets you create personalized video messages, slideshows and mini-movies. The app takes 360° selfies and lets the user add 10 different backgrounds, which include Riverfront, Millennium Falcon, Metropolis, Tea Garden and several others.

You can access and edit clips across iPhone X and iPad using iCloud. Videos are automatically uploaded and backed up to iCloud. You can start a video on iPhone X and finish it using your iPad.

Millennium Falcon scene

Tea Garden

Add text to your movie

There are lots of stickers and emoticons to add

7 The Standard Apps

iPhone X comes pre-installed with a core set of applications (apps), which make it so versatile and useful. In this chapter we explore some of the apps that haven't been covered in other chapters and show how to get the best use out of them.

Calendar

For those who want to get organized – people in business, education and many other sectors – the core Apple applications are: Calendar, Mail, Contacts, Phone and Notes.

These apps integrate well with each other on the iPhone and also on Mac computers with the same apps.

Setting up Calendar

Before you start entering data into Calendar, there are one or two settings you should check:

Make sure your time zone is set correctly or all of your appointments will be incorrect.

 Go to **Settings** > **Calendars**

 Tap **Time Zone Override** to override the automatic time zone

 Choose what to **Sync** with iCloud. (Do you want all events or just those for the past two weeks, month, three months, or six months?)

4 Set your **Default Calendar** – when you make new appointments using Calendar, this is where the appointments will be added. (You can add to another calendar quite easily, though)

Turn Calendars **On** in iCloud (**Settings** > **iCloud**) to ensure your calendar events are saved to iCloud and so will be available on other iCloud-enabled devices.

5 You can also set up **Start Week On**, **Default Alert Times** and other settings from here

---

14:31

‹ Settings   **Calendar**

ALLOW CALENDAR TO ACCESS

Siri & Search
Search & Siri Suggestions, Find in Apps ›

Time Zone Override   Off ›

Alternative Calendars   Off ›

Week Numbers

Show Invitee Declines

Sync   All Events ›

Default Alert Times   ›

Start Week On   ›

Default Calendar   Lectures ›

Location Suggestions

Calendar Views

To start using Calendar:

 1   Tap the **Calendar** icon to open the app

2   You will see the **Month View** – if it opens in **Day** or **List**, tap on the **Month** name at the top of the screen. This shows an overview of the month

 3   A gray dot means you have an appointment on that day, but it does not tell you how long the appointment is or what it is. Tap on the dot and you will see what the day's appointments are

4   If you need a detailed view of your appointments, check out the **Day** view (see next page)

Back to Year view

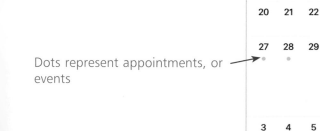

Dots represent appointments, or events

> **Hot tip**
>
> The Calendar uses continuous scrolling to move through Month view. This means you can view weeks across different months, rather than just viewing each month in its entirety; i.e. you can view the second half of one month and the first half of the next one in the same calendar window.

> **Hot tip**
>
> Tap on the **Today** button to view the calendar for the current day. From Day view, tap on the month button in the top left-hand corner to go to Month view. Tap on a date within the month to view it, with the days for the corresponding week at the top of the window. Swipe left and right on this to move between different weeks.

...cont'd

5 Tap on the **Today** button to view the calendar for the current day (tap on the red dot in Month view to go to that day). From Day view, tap on the month button in the top left-hand corner to go to Month view

To add more calendars, tap on the **Calendars** button and then the **Edit** button. Tap on the **Add Calendar** button at the bottom of the window and enter the required details.

6 Tap on a date within the month to view it, with the days for the corresponding week at the top of the window. Swipe left and right on this to move between different weeks

7 Tap on the **Calendars** button at the bottom of the window to view the available calendars

8 Tap on the **Inbox** button to view any invitations that you have been sent

9 Tap on the **List** button to view a scrollable list of all of your events

Searching Calendar

It's very easy to find appointments using the Search function within Calendar. You can also use the iPhone Spotlight search to find appointments.

 1   Tap **Calendar** to open the app

2   Tap on the **List** button

You can also search quickly for keywords in the Calendar using the search tool.

3   Scroll through the appointments and then tap an appointment to see its details

You can search your calendar using the inbuilt search tool, or use Spotlight.

Spotlight search

You can also search for appointments using the iPhone Spotlight search. To do this:

 1   Swipe downwards anywhere on the Home screen to access the Spotlight search

2   Enter a search word or phrase. This will search over all of the content on your iPhone, including within Calendars

3   Tap on one of the entries under the **Events** heading in the search results

Adding Appointments

Setting up a new appointment

To create a new appointment, or event, in the Calendar app:

 Tap on this button **+** to create a new event or rotate iPhone X to Landscape mode, then press and hold on a time slot

When adding a location, the Calendar can suggest specific geographic locations, according to what you have entered. Tap on one of the suggestions to accept it as the location.

 Enter a title and a location for the event

 Drag the **All-day** button to Off to set a timescale for the event

 Tap on the **Starts** button and drag on the barrels to set the time at which the appointment will start

 Do the same for the **Ends** time of the appointment

6 Tap on the **Alert** button and select a time at which you want an alert about the appointment

14:36

‹ New Event   **Alert**

None

At time of event

5 minutes before

15 minutes before

30 minutes before

1 hour before

2 hours before

1 day before

2 days before

1 week before

You can also invite other people to an event using the Invitees button (scroll down the options on the screen in Step 2). People can also send you invites to events, in which case you will receive an invitation alert that will appear on the Home screen and also in the Notification Center. If you accept an invitation, it will be added to your calendar.

7 Tap on the **Calendar** button and select a calendar in which you would like the appointment to be included

14:36

‹ New Event   **Calendar**

• Working calendar   ✓

• Lectures

• Family

8 Tap on the **Repeat** button and select a time for when you want the appointment or event to be repeated. This is a good option for items such as birthdays

14:36

‹ New Event   **Repeat**

Never   ✓

Every Day

Every Week

Every 2 Weeks

Every Month

Every Year

Custom   ›

Set up your repeat items, such as birthdays and anniversaries.

Keeping Notes

It is always useful to have a quick way of making notes of everyday things, such as shopping lists, recipes or packing lists for traveling. On your iPhone, the Notes app is perfect for this function. To use it:

1 Tap once on the **Notes** app

2 Tap once on this button to create a new note

3 Enter text for the note

4 Tap once on this button to share (via Message or Mail, or any social media apps on your iPhone), copy or print a note

5 Tap once on this button to access the formatting toolbar ⊕. Tap once on the cross to close the toolbar

6 Double-tap on text and tap once on this button to access text formatting options

7 Tap once on this button to create a bulleted checklist. Enter text for the list

If iCloud is set up for Notes (**Settings** > **Notes**) then all of your notes will be stored here and will be available on any other iCloud-enabled devices that you have.

The first line of a note becomes its title when viewed in the list of all notes.

You can edit a note at any time by tapping on it once in the top-level folder and editing the text as required.

8 Tap once on this button to add a handwritten, or stylus-drawn, item or drawing

9 Select a drawing object at the bottom of the screen and draw on the screen. Tap once on the **Done** button. The drawing is added to the current note

10 You can now add photos or videos (from Photos app, or shoot the photo/video as you write the note)

Press and hold firmly on the keyboard in Notes to activate it as a trackpad. You can then swipe over it to move the cursor around the screen. This can also be done in the Mail and Messages apps.

Maps App

Maps is a great application – it can help you find where you currently are, where you want to go, help you plan the route, tell you which direction you are facing and where all the traffic is. To use maps:

Open Maps; you are here

Tap the blue circle to view details

Press and hold to drop a pin

Satellite 3D view

Standard Apps

Don't forget

...ps will only work ...ith its full functionality if **Location Services** is switched **On** in **Settings** > **Privacy** > **Location Services**.

Hot tip

To see which way you are facing, tap the navigation arrow (bottom left) until it shows a blue beam around the blue circle.

Hot tip

Satellite view can also be used for the Flyover feature, or Flyover Tour, if this is available for the selected area.

Finding a route

Maps will calculate a route. It will also tell you how long it will take by car, public transport or on foot.

 Open the Maps app – your location will be shown

 Type a destination location or address into the box marked **Search for a place or address**

 Tap **Directions**

4 The route is shown on the map

 Choose your method of transport from the buttons along the bottom of the screen: Drive, Walk, Transport (public transport), and Ride (for ride booking apps if they are available in your area)

6 Tap on the **Go** button to get directions

7 The route is shown on the map with directions for each section. As you follow the directions they will change for the next step of the journey

Voice guidance is automatically turned On in Maps. If you want to change the volume, or turn the volume Off, you can do this in the Control Center (see page 28).

The Google Maps app is a good alternative that can be downloaded to your iPhone X. It includes voice-guided, turn-by-turn navigation, live traffic conditions and information on public transport. Google claims to constantly keep the "map of the world" updated!

News

iPhone X is ideal for keeping up with the news, whether you are on the move or at home. This is made even easier with the News app, which can be used to collate news stories from numerous online media outlets, covering hundreds of subjects. To use it:

1 Tap once on the **News** app

2 Tap once on the **Get Started** button

3 Tap on news publications in which you are interested and then tap on the **Continue** button

4 Tap on the **Following** button on the bottom toolbar to view the publications that were added in Step 3

After tapping on the **Get Started** button in Step 2 you will be asked if you want email alerts for the news feeds that you select. Tap on **Sign Me Up** or **Not Now**, as required.

5 Tap on the **+ Browse** button to add more items

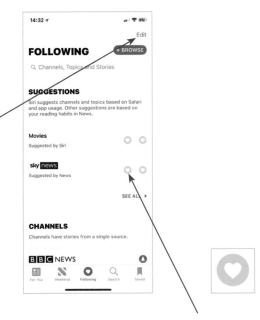

Tap on the **Edit** button to remove existing Favorite publications.

6 Select more publications or specific topics, by tapping on this button. These will be available under **Following**

7 When an article has been opened for reading, tap on this button 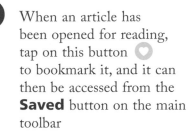 to bookmark it, and it can then be accessed from the **Saved** button on the main toolbar

8 The button second from left (as shown in Step 4) will either show Spotlight or Weekend depending on the day of the week. Opening this shows highlighted articles selected for you

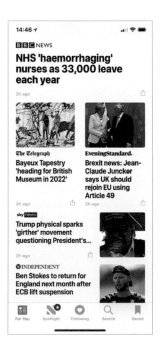

Tap on the **Search** button on the bottom toolbar to look for specific publications or subjects. These can then be added to your News feed and will appear under the **For You** and **Favorites** sections.

iBooks

The iBooks app can be used to download and read books on your iPhone.

 Tap on the **iBooks** app icon to view your library

Don't forget you can add your own PDFs and audiobooks to iBooks.

 Tap on the **Featured**, **Top Charts** or **Search** buttons to go to the iBooks Store

View, preview and download new books to read on your iPhone. These will be placed in the iBooks Library (above).

Health

The Health app in iOS 11 is designed to collect a range of health and fitness information such as body measurements, nutrition, fitness and sleep data. It can also be used in conjunction with other health and fitness apps from the App Store and aggregate information from these too. To use the Health app:

 Tap on this icon on the Home screen

 Use the buttons at the bottom of the screen to access the different sections

 Tap on the **Health Data** button to view the available categories

4 Tap on a category to view the options, then tap on an item on each page to select it and fill in the data as required

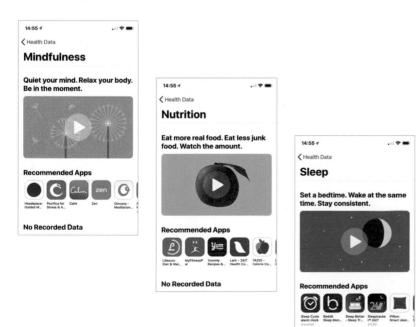

Check out our companion title, **iPhone & Apple Watch for Health & Fitness in easy steps**, in our online shop (**www.ineasysteps.com**).

Tap on the **Add Data Point** button within a category of the Health Data section to add the data for that item.

...cont'd

5 Tap on the **Vitals** button to view your pulse rate, blood pressure and other parameters

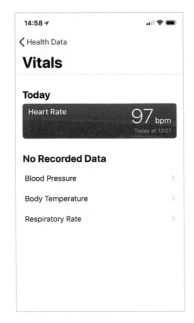

If you are concerned about any medical condition, always seek medical advice from your own doctor.

6 Tap on the **Sources** button (shown in Step 2 on the previous page) to view any apps that are accessing the Health app

7 Tap on the **Medical ID** button to add any important medical information such as medical conditions, blood type and allergies

Notification Center

Although the Notification Center feature is not an app in its own right, it can be used to display information from a variety of apps. These appear as a list for all of the items you want to be reminded about or be made aware of. Notifications are set up within the Settings app. To do this:

1 Tap on the **Settings** app

2 Tap on the **Notifications** tab

 Notifications

3 Tap on the items under the **Notification Style** section to add items to appear in the Notification Center, under the **Today** heading

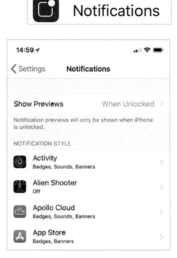

4 Drag the **Allow Notifications** button to **On** to enable the selected app to display notifications in the Notification Center

5 Select options for the notifications sound and icon, and select whether you want to show it on the Lock screen or not

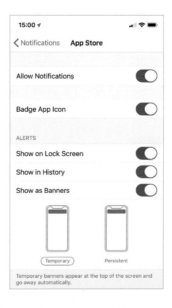

To enable email messages from your iCloud mail account to appear in the Notification Center, select the Mail app in Step 3 and tap on the **iCloud** button. On the next screen, drag the **Show in Notification Center** button to **On**.

...cont'd

Once the Notification Center settings have been selected, it can be used to keep up-to-date with all of your important appointments and reminders. It can also be used to display the weather for your current location. To view the Notification Center from any screen:

1 Drag down from the top left of any screen to view the Notification Center. The items in your Notification Center will be shown in chronological order, starting with the most recent at the top

2 Swipe up the page to view all of the items. Tap on one to open it in its own default app

Swipe up on the white bar at the bottom of the screen to close the Notification Center.

3 To delete a notification swipe it to the left then tap **Clear**

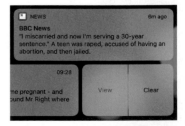

8 Working with Apps

There are tens of thousands of apps for iPhone X, catering for every conceivable need. This chapter looks at how to find apps in the online App Store, install them, update them and remove them.

Organizing Apps

When you start downloading apps you will probably soon find that you have dozens if not hundreds of them. You can move between screens to view all of your apps by swiping left or right with one finger.

To move an app between screens, tap and hold on it until it starts to jiggle and a cross appears in the corner. Then drag it to the side of the screen. If there is space on the next screen the app will be moved there.

138

As more apps are added it can become hard to find the apps you want, particularly if you have to swipe between several screens. However, it is possible to organize apps into individual folders to make using them more manageable. To do this:

1   Press on an app until it starts to jiggle and a cross appears at the top-left corner. (This can be used to delete the app unless it is a pre-installed app, in which case the cross does not appear)

2   Drag the app over another one

3 A folder is created, containing the two apps. The folder is given a default name, usually based on the category of the apps

4 Tap on the folder name and type a new name if required

Only top-level folders can be created; i.e. sub-folders cannot be created. Also, one folder cannot be placed within another.

139

5 Click on the **Done** button on the keyboard or swipe up from the bottom of the screen to finish creating the folder

6 Click the **Done** button again to return to the Home screen or swipe up the screen from the bottom

If you want to rename an app's folder after it has been created, tap and hold on it until it starts to jiggle. Then tap on the folder name and edit it as in Steps 4 and 5.

7 The folder is added on the Home screen. Tap on it to access the items within

About the App Store

While the built-in apps that come with the iPhone are flexible and versatile, it really comes into its own when you connect to the App Store. This is an online resource and there are over a million apps there that can be downloaded and then used on your iPhone, including categories from Lifestyle to Travel and Medical.

To use the App Store, you must first have an Apple ID (see page 17). This can be obtained when you first connect to the App Store. Once you have an Apple ID, you can start exploring the App Store:

 Tap on the **App Store** app on the Home screen

 The latest available apps are displayed on the **Today** page of the App Store

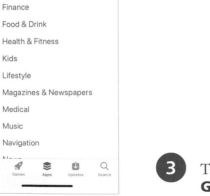

Tap on the **Apps** button at the bottom of the screen, then scroll down to **Top Categories** and click on the **See All** button to view apps in specific categories.

140

3 Tap on these buttons to view the apps according to **Games**, **Apps**, **Updates** and **Search**

...cont'd

Viewing apps

To view apps in the App Store and read about their content and functionality:

1 Tap once on an app

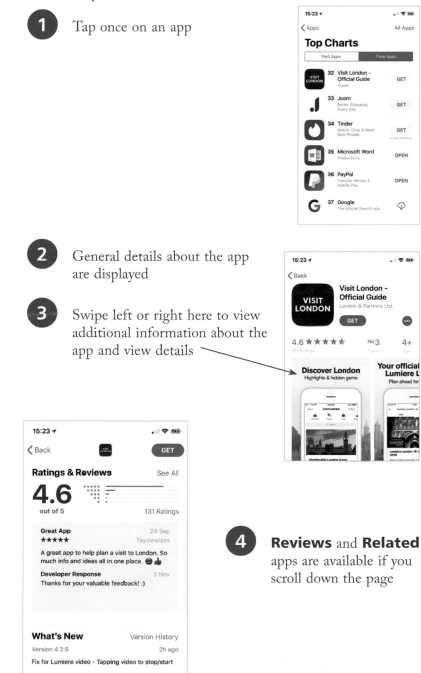

2 General details about the app are displayed

3 Swipe left or right here to view additional information about the app and view details

4 **Reviews** and **Related** apps are available if you scroll down the page

Finding Apps

Featured

Within the App Store, apps are separated into categories according to type. This enables you to find apps according to particular subjects. To do this:

 Tap on the **Apps** button on the toolbar at the bottom of the App Store

 Swipe left and right within categories, or click the **See All** button to view all apps in that category

 Scroll up the page to view additional categories

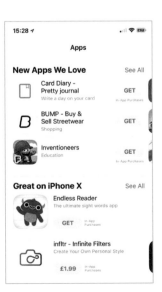

Top paid and free apps

To find the top rated apps:

 1 Tap on the **Apps** button on the toolbar at the bottom of the App Store screen

2 Scroll down till you see **Top Paid** and **Top Free**

3 To find the top apps in different categories, tap on the **See All** button. You will then see a tab marked **All Apps**. Tap this and categories are displayed

4 Select a category

5 The top apps for that category are displayed

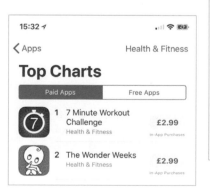

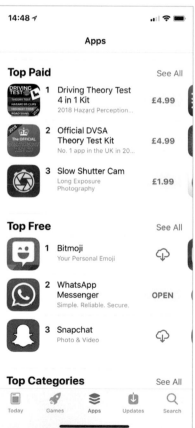

There are now so many apps, it may be difficult to find what you want. Try using the search tool and enter a word or words that describe what you are looking for.

Do not limit yourself to just viewing the top apps. Although these are the most popular, there are also a lot of excellent apps within each category.

Use the **Search** button on the bottom toolbar to look for specific apps using keywords.

143

Installation Process

To install apps from the App Store:

 1 Find the app you want using the **App Store** on the iPhone

 2 Tap the **Price** or **Get** tab

Make sure to remember your iTunes account password (your Apple ID) – you will be asked for this each time you try to install or update an app, even if it is free. Apps can also be bought using Apple Pay and Face ID, if this is set up.

 3 For free apps tap on the **Get** button

 4 You will then be prompted to double-click the side button to install

 5 The app will install

Updating Apps

The publishers of apps provide updates that bring new features and improvements to your existing apps. You don't have to check your apps to see if there are updates available – you can set them to be updated automatically through the Settings app. To do this:

1 Open **Settings** and tap on the **iTunes & App Store** link

🅐	iTunes & App Store	>

2 Drag the **Updates** button to **On** to enable automatic updates for apps

🅐	Updates	⬤

If your App Store icon has a red circle with a number inside, it means there's an update for one or more of your apps. If updates are not set to automatic, the apps can be updated manually in the **Updates** section of the App Store.

If you remove an app, it can be reinstalled from the App Store. The app will have a cloud icon next to it and will be free to reinstall, even if it was a paid-for app.

You can quickly see what apps you have, along with the date you last used them. Go to **Settings** > **General** > **iPhone Storage**. Scroll through the list and remove those you have not used for some time. You can also use the **Offload Unused Apps** option, but be careful if you use this action because you are allowing the iPhone X to remove apps you have not used. You may have upgraded your iPhone and transferred your apps, and because you have not used the app on your new iPhone it may be an app you use regularly. Once removed, the app's data will be removed too. It is better to remove apps yourself one by one.

Removing Apps

To remove apps from your iPhone (excluding pre-installed ones):

1 **Press and hold** the app you want to remove

2 All the apps on the screen will start jiggling and you will see an **x** at the top of the app unless it cannot be removed; i.e. it is a pre-installed app such as Phone, Mail, Calendar, etc. (see page 19)

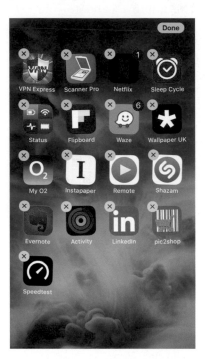

3 Tap the **x** to delete the app

4 Tap on the **Delete** button to confirm your action

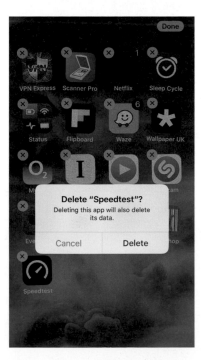

9 Web Browsing

Browsing the web on iPhone X is very easy using Apple's inbuilt browser, Safari. This chapter looks at how to use Safari, navigate around web pages and save and organize bookmarks.

Network Connections

Your iPhone can download data, such as emails and web pages, using a number of different types of connection. Some types of connection are faster than others. In general, Wi-Fi and Bluetooth should be kept Off if you are not using them because they use a considerable amount of power.

GPRS
This is a slow network! But often better than nothing.

EDGE
This is a relatively slow connection but is fine for email.

3G and 4G
These are faster connections than EDGE. 4G is pretty close to Wi-Fi speed.

Wi-Fi connection
Joining a wireless connection will give you fairly fast download speeds. There are many free Wi-Fi hotspots. You can use home Wi-Fi once you enter the password.

Bluetooth
This is a short-range wireless connection, generally used for communication using a Bluetooth headset.

What do the various icons mean?
Look at the top of the iPhone and you will see various icons relating to cellular and other networks.

Wi-Fi and Bluetooth drain battery power. Switch Off when not required.

●●●●●	Signal strength
O2-UK	Network provider
📶	Wi-Fi On, with good signal strength
✳	Bluetooth On
✈	Airplane mode On
☀	iPhone is busy connecting, getting mail, or another task that has not completed

Configuring Networks

Wi-Fi

 Go to **Settings** > **Wi-Fi**

 Tap **On** if it is off

 Choose a **network** from those listed and enter the password

 Tap **Ask to Join Networks** if you want to be prompted each time a new network is found. It's generally easier to leave this **Off**

 If you want to forget the network (e.g. maybe you have used one in a hotel), tap the name of the network you have joined, and tap **Forget This Network**

Use Wi-Fi when available to save using your data from the network provider.

10:48 ⚓

‹ Settings **Wi-Fi**

Wi-Fi ⬤

✓ VM1692178 🔒 🖵 ⓘ

CHOOSE A NETWORK...

HP-Print-B7-Officejet Pro X451dw 🔒 🖵 ⓘ

Lord of the Manor 🔒 🖵 ⓘ

Other...

Ask to Join Networks ⬤

Known networks will be joined automatically. If no known networks are available, you will have to manually select a network.

10:48 ⚓

‹ Wi-Fi **VM1692178**

Forget This Network

Auto-Join ⬤

IPV4 ADDRESS

Configure IP Automatic ›

IP Address 192.168.0.31

Subnet Mask 255.255.255.0

Router 192.168.0.1

Renew Lease

DNS

Configure DNS Automatic ›

HTTP PROXY

Configure Proxy Off ›

Browse with Safari

The Safari app is the default web browser on the iPhone. This can be used to view web pages, save favorites and read pages with the Reader function. To start using Safari:

 1 Tap on the **Safari** app

When a page loads in Safari a blue status bar underneath the page name indicates the progress of the loading page.

 2 Tap on the Address Bar at the top of the Safari window. Type a web page address

https://www.nationaltrust.org.uk   ⊗   Cancel

 3 Tap on the **Go** button on the keyboard to open the web page

Go

Scroll up to the top of the page to activate the top Address Bar, and the bottom toolbar when you tap on the page.

 4 Or, suggested options appear as you type. Tap on one of these to go to that page

10:50 ⌁

nationaltrust.org.uk — Home | Natio ⊗   Cancel

Top Hit

Home | National Trust
nationaltrust.org.uk

Siri Suggested Website

National Rail Enquiries
nationalrail.co.uk

5 The selected web page opens in Safari

Tap the time at the top of the screen to move to the top of the web page (this works with text messages, and other apps like Facebook, too). This is called Fast Scrolling.

10:51 ⌁

🔒 nationalgeographic.com

POPULAR STORIES

The Science Behind the Meteor That Lit Up the North American Sky

6 Swipe up and down and left and right to navigate around the page

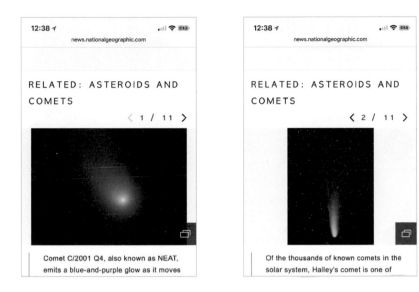

Double-tap with one finger to zoom in on a page by a set amount. Double-tap with one finger to return to normal view. If the page has been zoomed by a greater amount by pinching, double-tap with two fingers to return to normal view.

7 With thumb and forefinger, spread outwards to zoom in on a web page (pinch inwards to zoom back out)

You can also zoom in by placing your thumb and forefinger on the screen and pushing them apart (pinch them inwards to zoom out again).

You don't have to type ".com" or ".co.uk" for website addresses – simply hold down the "period" key and alternatives will pop up.

Navigating Pages

When you are viewing pages within Safari there are a number of functions that can be used:

Tap and hold on the **Forward** and **Back** buttons to view lists of previously-visited pages in these directions.

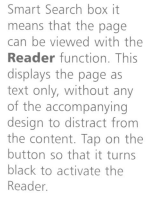

If a web page has this button in the Address Bar/ Smart Search box it means that the page can be viewed with the **Reader** function. This displays the page as text only, without any of the accompanying design to distract from the content. Tap on the button so that it turns black to activate the Reader.

1 Tap on these buttons to move forward and back between web pages that have been visited

2 Tap here to view bookmarked pages, Reading List pages and Shared Links

3 Tap here to add a bookmark, add to a Reading List, add to a note, add an icon to your iPhone Home screen, email a link to a page, Tweet a page, send it to Facebook or print a page

4 Tap here to add a new tab (see page 154), or press and hold to close all open tabs

5 Tap on a link on a page to open it. Tap and hold to access additional options, to open in a new tab, to add to a Reading List or to copy the link

6 Tap and hold on an image and tap on **Save Image** or **Copy**

Add Web Clips to the Home Screen

If you find a site that you want to revisit, but not add to Bookmarks, you can add it to the Home screen:

1 Open the required web page

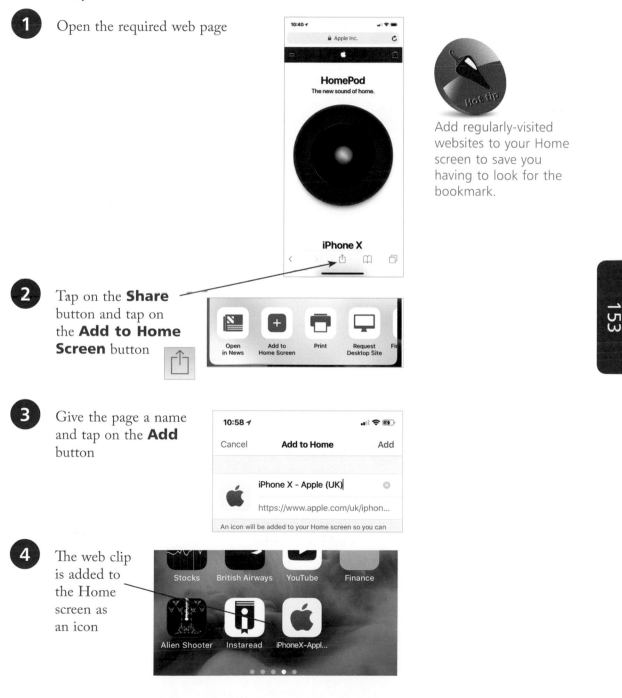

153

Add regularly-visited websites to your Home screen to save you having to look for the bookmark.

2 Tap on the **Share** button and tap on the **Add to Home Screen** button

3 Give the page a name and tap on the **Add** button

4 The web clip is added to the Home screen as an icon

Opening New Tabs

Safari supports tabbed browsing, which means that you can open separate pages within the same window and access them by tapping on each tab at the top of the page:

1 Tap here to view the open tabs

Tap and hold on the button in Step 1 for an option to close all tabs.

2 The open tabs are displayed. Tap on one to go to that tab

Tap on the **Private** button in the Tabs window to open a Private browsing session, where no web details will be recorded.

3 Tap on this button at the bottom of the window to create a new tab

4 Tap on the cross on a tab to close it

5 Open a new tab as in Step 3, entering a web address into the Address Bar, or tap on one of the thumbnails in the **Favorites** window

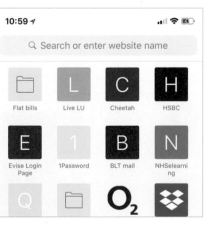

The items that appear in the Favorites window can be determined within **Settings** > **Safari** by tapping once on the **Favorites** link.

Bookmarking Pages

Once you start using Safari you will soon build up a collection of favorite pages that you visit regularly. To access these quickly they can be bookmarked so that you can then go to them in one tap. To set up and use Bookmarks:

 Open a web page that you want to bookmark. Tap here to access the sharing options

 Tap on the **Add Bookmark** button

 Tap on this link and select whether to include the bookmark on the Favorites Bar or in a Bookmarks folder

 Tap on the **Save** button

 Tap on the **Bookmarks** button

 Tap here on the **Bookmarks** button to view all of the bookmarks. The Bookmarks folders are listed. Tap on the **Edit** button to delete or rename the folders

Reading List and PDFs

The button in Step 5 on the previous page can also be used to access your Reading List and create PDFs.

Reading List

This is a list of web pages that have been saved for reading at a later date. The great thing about this function is that the pages can be read even when you are offline and not connected to the internet.

1 Tap on this button to view your **Reading List**

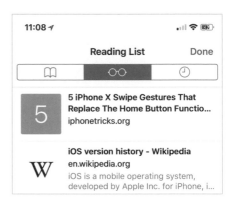

Creating PDFs

1 Navigate to web page from which you wish to create a PDF

2 Tap the **Share** icon then scroll to the right till you see **Create PDF**. Select this and choose location for the PDF

Reading List items can be added from the Share button in Step 1 on the previous page.

If you have accounts with Facebook or Twitter, you can link to these from their own headings within the **Settings** app. Once you have done this you can share content to these sites from apps on your iPhone.

Safari Settings

Settings for Safari can be specified in the Settings app. To do this:

1 Tap on the **Settings** app

2 Tap on the **Safari** tab

3 Tap on the **Search Engine** link to select a default search engine to use

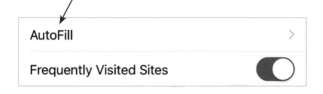

SEARCH	
Search Engine	Google >
Search Engine Suggestions	⬤
Safari Suggestions	⬤
Quick Website Search	On >
Preload Top Hit	⬤
About Search & Privacy...	

4 Tap on the default search engine you want to use with Safari, and return to Settings

Don't use **AutoFill** for names and passwords on any sites with sensitive information, such as banking sites, if other people have access to your iPhone.

5 Tap here for options for filling in online forms

AutoFill	>
Frequently Visited Sites	⬤

6 Tap on this button to access options for opening new links on a web site

Open Links	In New Tab >

7 Tap on this button to access options for the Favorites window that appears when you open a new tab

Favourites	Favourites >

...cont'd

 Switch **Ask Websites Not To Track Me** to **On**. Switching this on prevents websites recording your information

PRIVACY & SECURITY	
Prevent Cross-Site Tracking	
Block All Cookies	
Ask Websites Not To Track Me	

 Tap on the **Block All Cookies** link to specify how Safari deals with cookies from websites

Tap on **Clear History and Website Data** to remove these items

Clear History and Website Data

 Drag this button to **On** to enable alerts for when you are about to visit a fraudulent website

Fraudulent Website Warning

 Drag this button to **On** to block pop-up messages

Block Pop-ups

Cookies are small items from websites that obtain details from your browser when you visit a site. The cookie remembers the details for the next time you visit the site.

If the **History and Website Data** is cleared then there will be no record of any sites that have been visited.

(10) Email

Most of us spend a great deal of time reading and composing emails. This chapter looks at how to set up email on your iPhone X so that you can send and receive emails with your friends, family and colleagues.

Setting Up Email

The iPhone handles email well, and works with iCloud and Microsoft Exchange. It handles POP3 (seldom used today) and IMAP, and can work with Yahoo! Mail, Google Mail and AOL.

Setting up an email account

You can link to a variety of email accounts on the iPhone. This example uses a Gmail account:

The iPhone can handle many types of email account. IMAP accounts are useful since you can see all your folders on the server, and can save email to specific folders easily.

1 Go to **Settings > Accounts & Passwords**

2 Tap on the **Add Account** button

The iPhone X will automatically fetch or push emails from the relevant provider at regular intervals. To change the intervals or to turn Push Off, go to **Settings > Accounts & Passwords** and tap **Fetch New Data**. Then, switch Push Off or change the Fetch options at the bottom of the screen.

3 Select the account you want to add (in this case, Google)

4 Enter the account details and tap on the **Next** button

5 Select the items you want to include in the account and tap on the **Save** button

If you set up an iCloud account you will automatically be given an iCloud email account.

Deleting an account

To delete an email account from your iPhone:

 Go to **Settings** > **Accounts & Passwords**

2 Tap on the account you want to delete

14:26

‹ Settings **Accounts & Passwords**

🔑 App & Website Passwords >

ACCOUNTS

iCloud
iCloud Drive, Mail, Contacts, Calendars and 7 more... >

QMUL
Mail, Contacts >

Gmail
Mail, Contacts, Calendars >

Add Account >

Fetch New Data Push >

3 In the account window, swipe down to the bottom of the screen and tap on the **Delete Account** button and then the **Delete from My iPhone** button

13:41

‹ Accounts **Gmail**

GMAIL

Account drewprovan@googlemail.com >

✉ Mail ⬤

🧑 Contacts ⬤

📅 Calendars ⬤

▬ Notes ◯

Delete Account

161

Using Exchange Server

Mail can collect email, and sync calendars and contacts using Microsoft Exchange Server, which is great news for businesses. To do this:

 Go to **Settings** > **Accounts & Passwords**

 Tap on the **Exchange** button

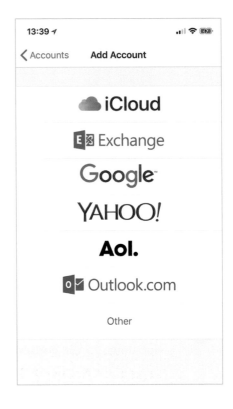

 Enter the details of your Exchange account (you may need to get these from your IT Administrator) and tap on the **Next** button

Email Viewing Settings

As with other apps, there are a number of settings for email:

1 Go to **Settings** > **Mail**

2 Tap on one of the accounts to view its settings

3 Adjust settings for **Preview**, **Ask Before Deleting**, **Show To/Cc Labels**, etc.

4 Access **Settings** > **General** > **Accessibility** > **Larger Text** to change the text size

If you want to see more text on the screen, set the font size to Small.

Composing Email

You can keep in touch with everyone, straight from the Mail app:

You can change your email signature, and even have different signatures for each email account. To change signature, go to **Settings** > **Mail** > **Signature**, then edit the signature. If you have multiple accounts you can change each one by selecting **Per Account**, then editing your signatures for each account.

To add documents to emails, press and hold on the subject area of the email and select **Add Attachment** from the pop-up menu. Select the required document from within the iCloud Drive and click on the **Done** button.

1 Tap the **Mail** icon to open the app

2 Tap an **email account** to open it

3 Tap the **New Email** icon (bottom right). A new email will open

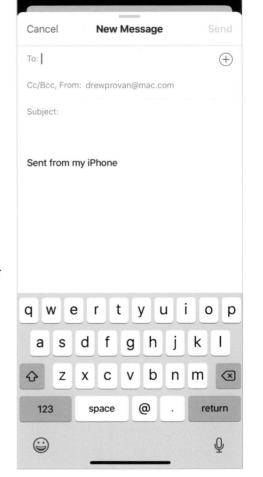

4 Tap the **To:** field and type the name of the recipient

5 Tap the **Subject:** and enter a subject for the email

6 Tap the **email body** area (below **Subject:**) and start typing your email

7 Insert a photo by pressing and holding in the body of the email and selecting **Insert Photo or Video** from the pop-up menu, and then select a photo from your photo gallery

8 Once complete, hit **Send**

Reading Email

When you receive email you can view it in the Mail app:

1 Check the **Mail** icon for fresh mail – represented by a red circle. The number refers to the number of unread emails

2 Tap **Mail** to open

3 Tap **All Inboxes** to access the email, and if there is blue dot next to an email it means that it is unread

4 If there is an attachment for the email this will be indicated by a paperclip icon next to it – you can tap to download

5 The attachment will appear in the body of the email. Tap on it to download it within the email

6 When the image attachment has finished downloading it will be visible in the body of the email

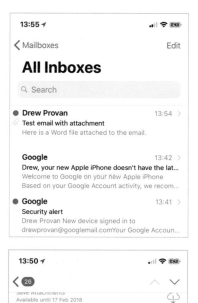

165

Flag important emails so you can find them again easily. Swipe from right to left on the email and tap on the **Flag** button.

Often, attachments do not download automatically. Tap the icon and you will see the attachment downloading. After downloading, tap to open.

To save documents, tap on the Share button and then tap on the relevant app to save within it; e.g. iBooks (to save PDFs), etc. To save a photo from an email, press and hold on the photo until you see **Save Image**. Tap on this, and the photo will be added to the **Photos** section of the **Photos** app.

Forwarding Email

Once you have received an email you can reply to the sender, or forward it to someone else:

1 Open an email

2 Tap the **Reply/ Forward** icon at the bottom right of the screen

3 Select **Forward**

Double-check that you have selected the correct button when forwarding an email, in case you are making comments about the original sender and accidentally **Reply** to them, rather than **Forward** to a new recipient.

4 Enter the name of the recipient in the **To:** box

5 In the body of the email, enter any message you want to accompany the forwarded email

6 Tap on the **Send** button

Deleting Email

You can delete email in a couple of different ways

1 Tap the email to read it

2 When finished, tap the trash icon at the bottom of the screen

Alternative method

1 In the email list view, slide your finger across the email from right to left (do not open it)

All Inboxes

Search

13:50 >   More   Flag   Delete

2 A red **Trash** (**Delete**) box should appear

3 Tap **Trash** (**Delete**) and the email will be deleted

There are also options in the slide feature to **Flag** the email and a **More** button, from which you can reply, forward, mark or move the email.

Yet another way of deleting email

1 Go to **All Inboxes** and tap the **Edit** button at the top right

< Mailboxes   All Inboxes   Edit

2 The contents of the Inbox are displayed in Edit mode

13:52 ⚡   .ıl 🌐 📳
                          Cancel
All Inboxes
Search
   Drew Provan   13:50
   Test email with attachment

3 Tap each email you want to delete and a blue circle will appear in the left-hand column

4 Hit **Trash** (**Delete**), in the bottom right-hand corner, when you are ready to delete

13:52 ⚡   .ıl 🌐 📳
                          Cancel
2 Selected
Search
   Drew Provan   13:50
✓ Test email with attachment

   Google   13:42
   Drew, your new Apple iPhone doesn't have t...
   Welcome to Google on your new Apple
   iPhone Based on your Google Account activ...

● Google   13:41
✓ Security alert
   Drew Provan New device signed in to
   drewprovan@googlemail.comYour Google A...

Moving Email to Folders

If you have an IMAP account, such as an iCloud account, you can see your folders on the server. You can move mail from your Inbox to another folder. This helps keep your mail organized, and your Inbox uncluttered.

Avoid having an Inbox full of read and new mail. Create folders for various categories of email within your IMAP account and move items to folders (easy with IMAP accounts) or delete them.

 Open the email you want to move, and tap on the **Folder** button on the bottom toolbar

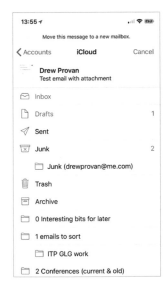

 Tap on the folder into which you want to move the email. In this instance, it is **0 Interesting bits for later**

 The email appears in the selected folder

0 Interesting bits fo...

🔍 Search

📎 **Drew Provan**   13:54 >
Test email with attachment
Here is a Word file attached to the email.

11 Accessibility Settings

iPhone X is well suited for people with visual or motor issues. This chapter details the Accessibility options on iPhone X, so that everyone can get the most out of it.

Accessibility Settings

Many people with visual, hearing or motor issues should be able to make use of devices like iPhone X. With the standard default configuration they may run into problems, but the iPhone has many settings that can be modified to make them more usable.

What features are available?

- VoiceOver
- Zoom
- White on Black
- Mono Audio
- Speak Auto-text

Most of these features will work with most applications, apart from VoiceOver, which will only work with the iPhone's standard (pre-installed) applications.

1 Tap on the **Settings** app

2 Tap on the **General** tab

General

3 Tap on the **Accessibility** link

Accessibility >

4 The **Accessibility** options are displayed – tap on a link to access more options

15:42

< General   **Accessibility**

VISION

VoiceOver   Off >

Zoom   Off >

Magnifier   Off >

Display Accommodations On >

Speech   >

Larger Text   Off >

Bold Text

Button Shapes

Increase Contrast   >

Reduce Motion   Off >

On/Off Labels

Face ID & Attention   >

5 Or, drag the button **On** or **Off** to access these

 6 Swipe up and down the page to view the full range of options for each item

VoiceOver

VoiceOver
This speaks what's on the screen, so you can tell what's on the screen even if you cannot see it. It describes items on the screen and, if text is selected, VoiceOver will read the text.

Speaking rate
This can be adjusted using the settings.

Typing feedback
VoiceOver can provide this: go to **Settings** > **General** > **Accessibility** > **VoiceOver** > **Typing Feedback**.

Languages
VoiceOver is available in languages other than English (but is not available in all languages).

VoiceOver gestures
When VoiceOver is active, the standard touchscreen gestures operate differently. Apple has listed the extensive range of gestures used with this setting. The URL for these is given below.

Apple Support for VoiceOver
See:
https://www.apple.com/voiceover/info/guide/_1131.html#vo27992

Activate Settings on iPhone X

Switching on VoiceOver

 Go to **Settings** > **General** > **Accessibility**

 Activate **VoiceOver** as shown below

3 When finished, you may wish to switch it off again

Tap on VoiceOver and drag the button On to activate it

Switch to Zoom to enlarge (Zoom cannot be used with VoiceOver)

Zoom

The iPhone touchscreen lets you zoom in and out of elements on the screen. Zoom will let you magnify the whole screen, irrespective of which application you are running.

Turn Zoom On and Off

1. Go to **Settings** > **General** > **Accessibility** > **Zoom**

2. Tap the Zoom **Off/On** switch

3. You cannot use Zoom and VoiceOver at the same time

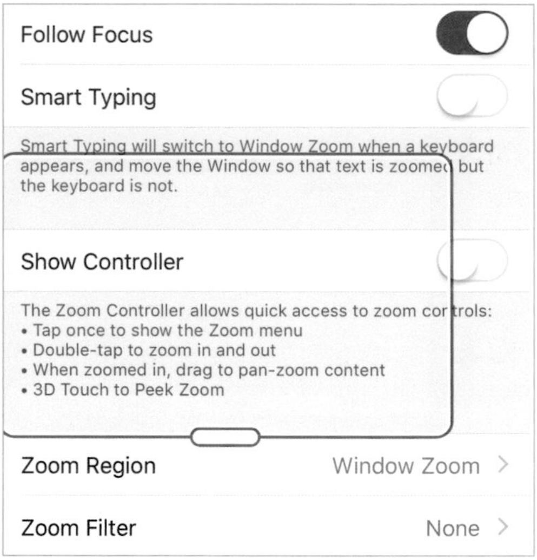

Follow Focus
Smart Typing
Smart Typing will switch to Window Zoom when a keyboard appears, and move the Window so that text is zoomed but the keyboard is not.
Show Controller
The Zoom Controller allows quick access to zoom controls:
• Tap once to show the Zoom menu
• Double-tap to zoom in and out
• When zoomed in, drag to pan-zoom content
• 3D Touch to Peek Zoom
Zoom Region
Window Zoom
Zoom Filter
None

Don't forget

To increase the overall text size on your iPhone, select **Settings** > **Accessibility** > **Larger Text**.

Zoom in and out

1. Double-tap the screen with three fingers

2. The screen will then magnify by 200%

Working with magnification

1. Double-tap with **three fingers** and drag to the top of the Zoom window (increase magnification) or bottom (decrease magnification)

2. Drag with **three fingers** to move around the Zoom window

Other Accessibility Settings

Activate Increase Contrast

This feature enhances the contrast on the iPhone, which may make it easier for some people to read.

 Go to **Settings** > **General** > **Accessibility**

 Tap the **Increase Contrast** link

 Drag the **Reduce Transparency** button to **On**

Turn Mono Audio On and Off

This combines the sound of both left and right channels into a mono audio signal played through both sides.

 Go to **Settings** > **General** > **Accessibility**

 Switch On **Mono Audio**

Turn Speak Auto-text On

This setting enables the iPhone to speak text corrections and suggestions as you type text into the iPhone.

 Go to **Settings** > **General** > **Accessibility**

 Select **Speech** > **Typing Feedback** > **Speak Autotext**

 Speak Auto-text works with both VoiceOver and Zoom

Large phone keypad

The keypad of the iPhone is large, making it easy for people who are visually impaired to see the digits.

 Tap the **Phone** icon (on the dock)

 Tap the **Keypad** icon (4th icon from left)

Closed Captioning (**Settings** > **General** > **Accessibility** > **Subtitles & Captioning** (under Media) > **Closed Captions + SDH**) adds subtitles to video content. Not all videos contain Closed Captioning information but where it is available you can access it by turning on Closed Captions.

Restrictions

If children are going to be using your iPhone, or if they have their own, you may want to restrict the type of content they can access:

1 Tap on the **Settings** app

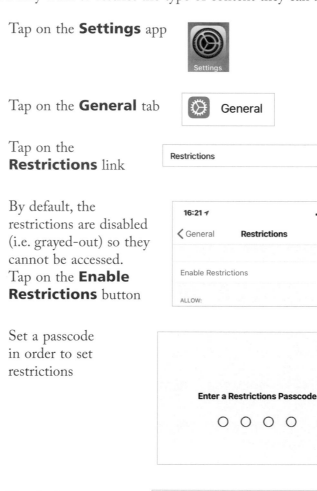

2 Tap on the **General** tab

General

3 Tap on the **Restrictions** link

Restrictions   Off >

4 By default, the restrictions are disabled (i.e. grayed-out) so they cannot be accessed. Tap on the **Enable Restrictions** button

16:21

< General   **Restrictions**

Enable Restrictions

ALLOW:

5 Set a passcode in order to set restrictions

Enter a Restrictions Passcode

○ ○ ○ ○

If you are restricting items for someone, make sure that you discuss it with them and explain your reasons for doing this, rather than just letting them find out for themselves when they try to use an app.

6 For the items you want to restrict, drag their buttons to **Off**. These icons will no longer appear on the iPhone's Home screen

15:57

< General   **Restrictions**

Disable Restrictions

ALLOW:

Safari

Camera

Siri & Dictation

FaceTime

12 Solving Problems

iPhone X occasionally misbehaves – an app will not close, or the iPhone may malfunction. This section looks at how to fix common problems and provides some helpful websites. The chapter also helps you find your lost or stolen iPhone X.

General iPhone Care

The iPhone is a fairly robust gadget but, like any complex piece of electronic hardware, it may suffer from knocks, scratches, getting wet and other problems.

Cleaning the body and screen

The best way to clean an iPhone is with a lint-free cloth such as the one below used for cleaning reading glasses. You can also use professional lens wipes, sold in most supermarkets. Make sure there is no grit or sand on the body or screen, and gently rub with the cleaning cloth. This should bring back the shine without scratching the glass or the body of the phone.

Paper kitchen towel, dampened with a little water containing a couple of drops of dishwashing liquid, is great for getting rid of heavily greased screens.

A glass protector is an excellent option for the iPhone screen.

Occasionally, the screen may get very greasy and a little soap helps to get the grease off

 Put a few drops of dishwashing liquid in warm water

 Get some paper kitchen towel and dip this into the water

 Wring out the kitchen towel so it is not dripping wet, and lightly wipe over the screen and rest of the casing

 Dry off using a clean cloth

Keep iPhone X Up-to-Date

Apple releases updates to the iPhone operating system periodically.

Is your iPhone X fully up-to-date?

1 Tap on the **Settings** app

2 Tap on the **General** tab

⚙ General		>

3 Tap on the **Software Update** link to view the current status of your operating system

10:30 ⏱   .ıll 🔺 🔋

‹ Settings   **General**

About   >

Software Update   >

4 If there is an update available it will be displayed

5 Tap on the **Download and Install** button

No SIM 🔺   11:33   ⏱ ✻ 6% ▭ ⚡

‹ General   **Software Update**

iOS 11.2.2
Apple Inc.

About 26 seconds remaining

iOS 11.2.2 provides a security update and is recommended for all users.

For information on the security content of Apple software updates, please visit this website:
https://support.apple.com/en-gb/HT201222

Downloading...

Software updates for iPhone users are provided free by Apple. If one becomes available, download and install it.

Rather than updates yourself, iPhone X can update automatically for you. Go to **Settings > iTunes & App Store** and make sure **Updates** has been switched On.

🅰 Updates	🔘

You can conserve battery power by switching off Wi-Fi and Bluetooth. Instead of opting for push email, you can check for email manually (see page 160).

Consider using Airplane mode (**Settings** > **Airplane Mode**) for conservation of power. However, you will not be able to make or receive any calls, texts or notifications (see page 29).

The display brightness can also be altered from within the Control Center (swipe down from the top right of the screen).

Maximize iPhone X Battery

iPhone is a bit of a power hog. Browsing the web, listening to music and watching videos drains significant amounts of power. If you only make a few phone calls each day, your iPhone will last a couple of days between charges. But most people use it for far more than this, and their battery will last about a day.

Tweaks to ensure maximum battery life

 Switch off **Wi-Fi** if you don't need it

 Switch off **Bluetooth** if you don't need it

 Battery Percentage is on by default with iPhone X. To see the percentage go to the Control Center

Use a lower cellular speed (e.g. 3G instead of 4G) under **Settings** > **Mobile Data** > **Mobile Data Options** > **Enable 4G**

 Collect your email manually, under **Settings** > **Accounts & Passwords**. Tap **Fetch New Data** then select **Push, Fetch** or **Manual**

Set **Auto-lock** to a short period (e.g. 1 minute) under **Settings** > **Display & Brightness**

 Reduce the brightness of your screen, under **Settings** > **Display & Brightness**

 Press the **Off** button once when you have finished using the iPhone (this is Sleep mode, which uses less power)

Restart, Reset & Hard Reset

Restart the iPhone

 Hold down the **On/Off** and **Volume Down** buttons

 When you see the **Slide to Power Off** appear, swipe this to the right

 Leave the iPhone for a couple of minutes then press the **On/Off** button again and let the phone restart

The On/Off button is also used for the Sleep/Wake function.

Quit an app
Sometimes apps freeze or misbehave and you'll want to quit and reopen them. To do this:

 Drag your finger from bottom of the screen to the middle. You should see the running apps

 Touch and hold your finger on one app until a **red minus** sign appears next to each app. Tap the minus for the app you wish to quit or flick the app upwards

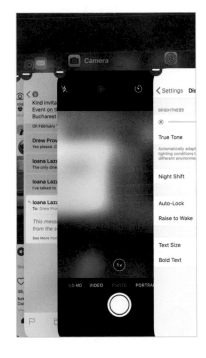

Force Quit the iPhone

 Press and quickly release the **volume up** button, then press and quickly release the **volume down** button

 Now press and hold the **side button** until iPhone X restarts and the Apple logo appears

...cont'd

Before doing a reset, back up your iPhone X to ensure you do not lose any data when you restore the iPhone (see pages 62-64).

The **Reset Home Screen Layout** option returns your Home screen to the way it was when you first got your iPhone.

Resetting the iPhone

There are various aspects of your iPhone that can be reset to their factory defaults. These include resetting the Home screen layout, network settings and the keyboard dictionary. You can also reset all of the settings on the iPhone, or erase the content and settings. This erases all of the content and resets the iPhone to its factory, unused, condition. You may want to do this if you have been using the iPhone and then want to give it to someone else. To do this:

 Select **Settings > General** and tap on the **Reset** button (at the bottom of the page)

Reset	>

 All of the Reset options are displayed. Tap on the **Erase All Content and Settings** button

10:53 ✈   ·ıl 🛜 ▪️

‹ General   **Reset**

Reset All Settings

Erase All Content and Settings

Reset Network Settings

Reset Keyboard Dictionary

Reset Home Screen Layout

3️⃣ Enter the passcode, if you use one to lock your iPhone

Enter Passcode   Cancel

Enter your passcode

○ ○ ○ ○ ○ ○

4 Tap on the **Erase iPhone** button

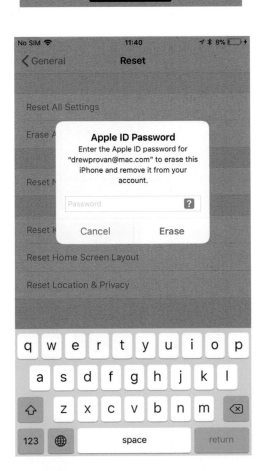

Reset Home Screen Layout

Reset Location & Privacy

This will delete all media and data, and reset all settings.

Erase iPhone

Cancel

5 Since it is a serious action, you will be asked if you are sure. Tap on the **Erase iPhone** button again

6 Enter your Apple ID and tap on the **Erase** button to return your iPhone to its factory condition

No SIM   11:40   8%

< General   **Reset**

Reset All Settings

Erase A

Apple ID Password
Enter the Apple ID password for "drewprovan@mac.com" to erase this iPhone and remove it from your account.

Reset N

Password   ?

Cancel   Erase

Reset K

Reset Home Screen Layout

Reset Location & Privacy

q w e r t y u i o p
a s d f g h j k l
⇧ z x c v b n m ⌫
123 🌐 space return

If you reset the contents and settings for your iPhone you can restore them when you next turn on the phone. This can be done from an iCloud or an iTunes backup and is done at the **Set Up iPhone** step of the setup process.

183

Apple Resources

Visit Apple!

The first place you should look for help is the Apple site. After all, iPhone X is their creation so they should know more about it than anyone.

The iPhone and iPhone Support areas are packed with information, tutorials and videos.

Useful URLs

http://www.apple.com/iphone/

http://www.apple.com/support/iphone/

David Pogue's posts

David Pogue is always worth reading – he loves technology and loves all things Apple. Try his own website at:

http://davidpogue.com/

iLounge.com

iLounge has long provided loads of hints and tips for Apple devices. They review hardware and accessories, and provide reviews of new gear for the iPhone, the iPad and the iPod.

What's on iPhone (whatsoniphone.com)

Largely a review site but it also provides information about hardware and for people interested in developing for the iPhone.

The first place to look for hints, tips and fixes, if you can't find them within this book, is Apple's website, which is full of information and videos.

184

If You Lose Your iPhone

If you have lost or misplaced your iPhone, you can use iCloud to look for its location. The iPhone has to be on and transmitting to the cellular network in order for Find My iPhone to work.

Find My iPhone also allows you to erase the entire contents of your iPhone remotely. This means that if it gets stolen, you can remotely erase the iPhone and prevent whoever stole your iPhone from getting their hands on your personal data.

Set up Find My iPhone
Before you use Find My iPhone it has to be set up. To do this:

 Within **Settings** tap on the **iCloud** tab

 Tap on the **Find My iPhone** link and if the **Find My iPhone** functionality is Off, drag the button to **On**

If for no other reason, it is worth getting an iCloud account so you can track your iPhone and erase the contents if it gets stolen.

 Tap on the **OK** button in the Find My iPhone dialog box to activate this functionality

Find My iPhone Enabled

Find My iPhone allows you to locate, lock or erase your iPhone if it's lost or stolen. It will also be enabled on any paired Apple Watch or supported accessory that uses your Apple ID.

OK

Locating your iPhone
Once you have set up Find My iPhone, you can then use the online service to locate it, lock it, or erase its contents.

 Log in to iCloud (**www. icloud.com**) from a PC or other Apple device

 Click on the **Find iPhone** button

...cont'd

The **Play Sound** option is a good one if you have lost the iPhone in your own home.

If you are using Apple Pay, this will be deactivated if you click on the **Lost Mode** button in Step 8. This is a good security measure if you lose your iPhone.

Click on the **Erase iPhone** > **Erase** button if you are worried that someone might compromise the data on your iPhone.

 To use the Find My iPhone functionality you have to sign in again with your Apple ID

 The location of your iPhone is shown on a map

 Click on the **i** symbol to see options for your lost iPhone

 Details about the phone, and options for what you can do, are displayed

7 Click on the **Play Sound** button to send an alert sound to the phone. A message is displayed to let you know that a sound has been sent to your iPhone

 Click on the **Lost Mode** button to lock your iPhone remotely. You have to enter a passcode to do this and this will be required to unlock the iPhone

Index

Q

R

S

T

U

V

W

Y

Z